HEMLOCK

HEMLOCK
Old Women in Bloom

HÉLÈNE CIXOUS

TRANSLATED BY BEVERLEY BIE BRAHIC

polity

First published in French as *Ciguë* © Éditions Galilée, 2008

This English edition © Polity Press, 2011

Polity Press
65 Bridge Street
Cambridge CB2 1UR, UK

Polity Press
350 Main Street
Malden, MA 02148, USA

ISBN-13: 978-0-7456-4867-5
ISBN-13: 978-0-7456-4868-2(pb)

A catalogue record for this book is available from the British Library.

Typeset in 10.75 on 14 pt Janson Text
by Servis Filmsetting Ltd, Stockport, Cheshire
Printed and bound in Great Britain by MPG Books Group Limited,
Bodmin, Cornwall

Every effort has been made to trace all copyright holders, but if any have been inadvertently overlooked the publisher will be pleased to include any necessary credits in any subsequent reprint or edition.

For further information on Polity, visit our website: www.politybooks.com

This book is supported by the French Ministry of Foreign Affairs as part of the Burgess Programme run by the Cultural Department of the French Embassy in London. www.frenchbooknews.com

Liberté · Égalité · Fraternité
RÉPUBLIQUE FRANÇAISE

CONTENTS

MAMA'S NOT IN MAMA — THERE'S SOMEONE ELSE

"Disappearance" I tell myself, I fled upstairs, "I've seen her – I saw it – " I threw myself into my study onto my desk, a raft moored to the edge of nothingness in the corner of the door, so I can't shut it, I always have this door standing open at my shoulder, but in another way if there's an alert, as was the case, two leaps and I'm at the emergency exit. Never had there been such a heap of ruins on my desk, to which I rapidly added, as one releases a sob, a sheet of paper painted with exclamations, arrows, words, not as I might have expected tightly packed, but stretched panicky thin as if the very words had been swept up in the state of flight and fought their way across the margins to the exit, with the result that the word *disappearances* is flattened over an entire line to the point of disappearing. Similarly the words *Very painful news* were stretched so thin that pppppppaainnn would be illegible to anyone but me – this depicts the feeling of interminability, of vanishing caused by the shock of terror, and the illusion of bottomlessness I must for a moment have felt and which had been triggered in my mother's room. I am streaming out of the abyss I tell myself. Envoy of disappearance, I flung this onto a yellow Post-it, where I'd jotted some other time: "It can't be very far away now." The two sentences seemed to echo one another, whereas they were unrelated. And that's how a piece of writing starts I thought, random combinations. I'd begun to think of "literature" as an object of astronomical observations, I thought of the secret way the greatest philosopher in the world my friend J.D. gets thrown in a nanosecond to the furthest reaches of thought by a word or two chanced upon at the top of a book by Hobbes

I began to pluck off the terrors whose six legs clung to my sleeves with their middle feet, my cardigan lapel, in front I had them on my thighs and this entire beast was squirming and clinging to me

Again I yanked off one of the sentences-terrors that stuck to me like one of those leeches of woeful memory applied to "my grandmother," Proust's grandmother, to help her defeat death, and those beasts instead of helping her helped death, but so it goes, everything one does against evil, evil feeds on and fattens on, already it demanded another mouthful and again I had to struggle to overcome my resistance before I could throw the phrase down on the paper thus: *ghosts are there*.

I could see perfectly well what it wanted to say, but I kept it at arm's length. I bolted upstairs to my bibliomortgaged life, into this retreat guarded by several lines of very powerful books, where my mental health is less directly exposed to the pressures of the imminences. I bolted. In the world-other, there are exits and escape hatches, and good hideouts everywhere. And there, I tell myself, by definition, no *disappearance*, just the opposite. Upstairs appearance is everything. Literature knows nothing but appearance.

Now that I've regained the initiative (and I'll not deny

having been surprised, and head on, by an attack that threw me completely off guard) it's up to me to try to think through this event, which, I admit, swept me away like a straw in the tornado. I will and I want to. I was in a hurry to transform the damage into a story. I admit *Ghosts st there* is a pre-title. As to title-in-waiting, *Dans*, that is, *In*, came right to mind. With a fountain pen, and not the felt-tip I use to scribble emergencies, I scrawled the word across the face of a folder. Finally I wrote it *Dents*, that is, *Teeth*. *Dans, Dents*: same difference. Later I'll put all the story's drafts into this envelope.

I will never be able to write that, I tell myself, I wrote, for it was true, I *could see* the problems, it's a borderline situation, the subjects of the story have been spirited away from themselves, and replaced in their absence by sorts of shades, and yet I tell myself, I will respect the moral duty of musician to audience, as my mother herself does daily, meticulously executing her piece, a model of obedience I can't do otherwise or better than to imitate. And even had I to submit myself to the tortures of writing-in-spite-of, for my mother's sake I'd do it. Worse things have been done. I see Proust prodding his narrator to report his grandmother's death throes, unadulterated horror, and assassination; still he yokes him to the task, and the narrator complies to the point of delirium. Now just today, something was awry in the perfect execution of the work that she knows and plays by heart, all of a sudden there was a blank; into this breach the pre-face of the last face was ominously sucked. All it took was one little hole. One must imagine an accident of sight, around eleven o'clock in the evening, a time of truce, which my mother and I never spend together.

I look at her.

I can't look at her, I look at her, I can't, I don't want to, I take my gaze in hand and pin it down, I clamp my teeth into its neck, I must, my gaze gazes at her, fast it wriggles away, I'm ashamed, what a mysterious crime not to *be able to* look at her, I mean to be in the grip of an impotence more potent than my will, a power failure more powerful than my straining to want to look at her, for within me is a religious, devoted being who enjoins me to look at her, I am rebuked, teeth in her nape I wrench my gaze back and for a second, maybe two, I look, what a sin, not to be able to want to look at her, to want to be able to look at her and not to be able to give this wanting strength enough to overcome the prodigious impotence whose muscles, in the distraught resistance that doesn't want to be able, redouble in strength, such sins, and still I don't give up, each time my gaze gazes away, I wrench it back, and during the violent minutes of this struggle, inside me, fear weeps, I'm ashamed, I accuse myself of a sort of treason that I didn't know hadn't known up to this second I could ever be the agent, the cause, the site of, never had I imagined such a test, to be measured, to see myself brought to the point of betraying the person who is more me than myself, to fight with all my strength so as not to see myself allowing myself to yield to the relief of flight

and without preparation, without warning, or perhaps there was something I didn't notice,

because why I am here, in mama's room, at a time of day when usually I'm sound asleep, will require an explanation in a moment, usually I sleep upstairs, "up there" as she says, what happened? my friend will ask. I sleep over mama, that is on mama, I venture off to the depths assured that all the same, downstairs, below, is the harbor, anchor, terra firma, well, this usual, guaranteed sleep was broken into, by what by whom my friend will ask, there was a blow, I was sleeping, the sleep opened, I ran, I can't swear I heard a cry in reality, I was on the stairs, barefoot in my nightgown, and it was *when* I opened the door that I *saw* her I mean that I saw the invisible, as one sees the invisible, my mother cried out, at the same

4

time as me, on the dot of that *when,* she opened her mouth
I saw the invisible, I cried out, our two names clung to one
another, hugging in the middle of the little room over the
void. "But what is this ghost?" my mother said, I saw mama's
fear. "Come here, come here!" I sat my fear down on the edge
of her bed.

The book is keeping me from reproducing the *exact* trace
of the event. I'm talking about a sheet of paper upon which, in
the dark, just before I flung myself into the stairwell, I jotted
a few testamentary words. One last gesture. I've seen this sort
of thing moments before a shipwreck, the great mad sailors
in Melville or Poe do this, as if they hoped, going off to their
deaths, to live on in the form of a scrap of paper without a
hope of not being sucked into the maelstrom. In the dark I
dashed off:

> *She's on the staircase*
> *I say & one doesnt see her*
> *Rather in th lane my mother says*
> *Be careful oh pls*
> *We , know*
> *This time we we are*
> *Side by side*
> *no holding back*
> *We are in complete agreement*

From the tangle of signs, askew, dashed off in five seconds,
one sees the grimace in the letters shattered as if pounded
again and again by huge waves. The awful thing about such
shipwreck experiences is the hateful ferocity of the waves,
sic, unda ibat in arma ratis multoque erat altior illis. Rima patet
praebetque viam letalibus undis, this is all that floats up from
Book XI of the *Metamorphoses* to my shore of the dead after

5

the storm has passed, and it's not without me clinging to each line, reading and struggling word by word, when I let one thread go I get it back at the rhyme but night falls over me, waves lift the text, which seems to merge with the sky.

"What's happening?" my mother cries. I see her eyes terrified by a wildness in mine, a fury, I see my cry in her eyes, but what's around her eyes, what's missing – I am searching. When I want to look at her, fish her back up, pull her out of a deathly water that holds her head clamped in its jaw, I can't bring myself to – *sic*

So, the water, throw, ropes, beyond me, greatly, fissures open within me, my ankles collapse

My gaze forks, flees. I look at "her, at it" there. The gaze flattens itself, creeps. I make myself. Whip. Gaze I-less, me-less, no one can do that. What's happening, don't let it happen, it's as if I were killing. I am not. *Mama is not in mama*. She has been replaced. I myself am decomposed. She hasn't been replaced. She hasn't had time. It's because I stormed in. Instead of mama, someone who's been standing in for her ever since she ceased to be herself, and that up to now she has managed to keep out of sight. No, that's not it. Maybe I should have banged on the door to her bedroom before I opened it. This is not her. Under my eyes, a distortion of the image of the person I will not be able not to look at when she will have left me I won't be able to take my eyes off her. It is absolutely forbidden to see what one will see. This is what has happened to me, by chance, through a misunderstanding, I thought, I rushed to help her, I threw open the door. And I saw. The state-of-God: a hole one can't look at without seeing death, I see it, my eyes turn to ash. The face to which my mother has come is a little piece of skin loosely basted to the bottom of the eyes, for one cannot call these insubstantial hems eyelids. My gaze fails us but I tame my body. We remain. I have seen her without her dentures. So, I say to myself, she knows. I've never seen her before alive without teeth, taken out, in her lifetime. So I tell myself *everything depends on the teeth*. What's this ghost here? So there are two mummies. One of them is mama, the other is the other her, the *aged* one. Never before had I seen *the Age*. I didn't know it was there, in her, she must have been its hostage, and not a peep, she's been hiding it, and since when? *Thus* I see who takes over when I'm not around. For me she slips her face on. Now I see how she dons her smile to come and see me up there. And here, in the grip of Age, she couldn't smile at me. Instead of the smile, the entrance to a little tomb. Across the slit of the entrance, a drapery of skin made up of a multitude of wrinkles. I have sat down beside mama and smiled at her. Never before had I seen that what I for years feared seeing was already present in my mother's room, had been there maybe since those same years when I used to believe I was upstairs keeping watch. At what a distance I'd kept from believing what I feared I already believed. Suddenly I'm afraid that I have done every-thing behind the back of my heart to avoid catching sight of the occupant. Every morning I go by this closed door, I have never let myself into the secret. As if I'd given the enemy a chance, allowed him a guilty, prudent tolerance. Not that I start up at the least creak. But whenever I burst in, I did so in the dark, on tiptoes, I didn't wake her, I didn't see the Age, I didn't wake myself. I never saw Disappearance in person. Still, if I refrained from any kind of breaking in, my mother never showed any desire to show me the state-of-emptiness-of-God either.

My soul turns to stone. Am I staring? I put a smile on my face. Mama's voice struggles, groans, hauls itself up.

– What were you doing up there?

– I was thinking about you. I thought you called me.

She is lying on her bed. I sense she is strangely content.

7

Perhaps not to have to pretend any more? Perhaps to see me tremble with love.

She starts her music again. She'd stopped the second I left her in front of the television, en tête-à-tête with her soap opera. Last movement.

– I watched my Derrick. That Derrick is only interested in people who disappear. And him, fifty years and still going strong. Éri tells me: I saw him in Israel fifty years ago. Nowadays his hair is white.

Something in my mother resists disappearance. Or maybe someone. Or maybe once people disappear they're no longer in danger of disappearing. Later on they turn up again in mama's conversation.

She dozes off. My left hand on her left arm over the patch of infected skin that never sleeps. Age and Illness keep their silent watch over her little body. With my right hand I pick up my notebook and I take a step against the silence

I write: "*She* is on the staircase"

I write, watching her – stroking: "Her head has shrunk again crumpled around the slit." Her hands grow larger. Her big eyelids. She opens her eyes. Ghost of a smile. Off again. Totally loved. I withdraw my left hand. She holds onto it. I detach my left hand by unscrewing it gently with my right hand starting with the wrist. Quickly I leave. *She* is on the staircase.

Maybe I should have begun this book with these words the last before the storm. One dies a thousand deaths each one covers up the one before.

The way I am hallucinated more and more, say I, possessed, says my friend. – Maybe it's the intensity? Could be age he says. – What if they told you it's not me I say it's someone else writing my books? In fact it is someone else. But who? *She is on the stairs*, the other. *She*, we say, my mother and I – we say *elle* – because we discuss this in French. Someone who wants at whatever price to make this book.

My brother saw it, or her, too, except in his case he was watching television, shortly before midnight. She noticed a light. Thought she'd left it on. Appeared. A specter says my brother. She was very surprised to see me. I saw a hundred-year-old crone. According to him the age of the face is a function of the mechanical structure of our bones and teeth. Take out the teeth and the jaws look atrophied the lower jaw is no size at all, you don't see the top of the face any more. When a third of the whole collapses, it creates a disharmony, what is above what is absent no longer looks normal. From the nose down, half of the face collapses and gets sucked into the empty mouth. The face swallows itself, whence the feeling of hallucination that stuns the witness. And quick! She closed the door. What staggers me is how well her dentures, modest though they are, do the job. The teeth a perfectly natural greyish white. She probably has a very precise vision of her dwindling longevity. When I go to the market with her, people say good morning, she doesn't answer, no longer asks for anything, people take her for an apparition, they look at her with surprise, underneath the apparition an aged being executes the old entrechats, swaying, she makes her way through the world. It looks much bigger than in the old days and utterly changed.

(Insert, after the market, *the song of return*, for two voices. In a major key, with lots of sun, lilting, my brother. The other, quavery. *The other*. – The market dazzled me. I no longer knew where I was. *Him*. – Tomahtoes! Rah-dish!

9

Quavery. – What? *Him.* – Rah-dish. Purring: Buh-ter-beans. *Her.* – The Rice! I knew it! It's not here! *Him.* – Let's unpack the bags first! Rahsp-berry! And . . . . Rice!)

She laughs. I feel down in the dumps. And if my brother too saw her – the other – I fear it's a bad sign. In her fight with the ghost, it may be that our mother is failing. I imagine her fatigued, struggling to keeping herself apart, to remember, to do her imitation, every morning, which would explain why she makes her entrance later and later, after she has managed to cobble together a sufficiently convincing resemblance. It may be that Age weakens her memory of the illusion she wants to go on giving us. Nor, I tell myself, can I say to her: relax, this would be as ill advised as the leeches. Nor can I ever know to which of them exactly my advice goes. I can't side with the older, for it's the younger, it's "mama" who infuses the other old woman, older and hoarier than her own mother ever was, with these fabulous remains of juvenility. Nor can I simply side with "mama," when out of the corner of my eye I glimpse the silhouette of a very old person tottering in her room, almost falling as she inches up the trousers whose legs hold the print of mama's nimbleness and speed. My brother and I exchange glances, and each murmurs: Alas, mama, how you are changed! See already you are no more neither two nor one

I too want to keep the illusion. In the morning I wait for mama to come up and take her shower. She comes later and later. I don't notice.

IN WHICH COUNTRY?

In which country? The visible invisible, the realm of the
dead, I say to myself, I've been there more than once, I tell
myself, without knowing it and without seeing it, naturally,
each time it's something else so how can you refer to it, I tell
myself – afterwards long afterwards, after many involuntary,
disconcerting trips, as if I were being loaned to that country,
or it loaned to me, or I lent myself, sadness accompanies my
arrival, the presentiment that I have no future there, but this
no-future I feel only when I return, the feeling I have no
entry there though I entered, finally, later I understand, when
I leave I am alone too, I return from afar and the memory of
the country doesn't come with me, it remains in the distance,
I am sad, with no place to live

And then there are the warnings, which I don't receive,
which I receive without receiving, unless with a shudder
of my entire being, those throbbing sounds that brush up
against me, I am a subject of wind and cold, wherever I go
words mock me, a cloak of winds enfolds me, two words chill

my heart with their bat-caress, especially should they whisper in a foreign language, it's an address, the address of the threshold, "Rendezvous in Lthwhrf." – What did you say? I called, standing on the rampart or maybe the railing, I lean out, as if the Voice might repeat the address, as if it were still there, down in the well of time, as if I could for once by crying out arrest Oblivion, as if the Dream having descended into Nothingness might be able to come back up in flesh and blood, and still I plead, if the   at this very moment, *still* I *know* I heard distinctly the address of the rendezvous, unfortunately it was at that very moment when the minty smell of daybreak sends dreams packing, dethrones the lords of night and sweeps them like beggars from day's arid terrains, just one second more and I'd have jotted it down, I even felt it flicker out at the edge, in my mouth, in the hollow of my ear, just time to grab a pencil, it seems to me that the words when I saw them in flesh and blood were four dream colors red white black and rome, it seems to me that in the middle there was a hinge, a kind of sonorous apostrophe, but I'm no longer all that sure, oh! if only I could go back but no reverse, no direction, *still* I've managed all the same to keep a pinch of sound even if I didn't catch the address, at least

it seems to me they proclaimed a resurrection, but it seems to me that in the words that got carried away there was a dark and gently paradoxical power, to call and at the same time forbid hearing as if it were necessary to follow them blindly, with the deaf and dumb submission of the dead, I should have slept on, dreamt, but I get up, I wreak havoc on myself

left behind, the empty chest, the triumphant and useless certitude that the key words had been given, that I hadn't the luck, or the right or the honor to possess them, or the time, or the strength, or the merit, but at least the trace of the disappearance had not been confiscated.

Lthwhrf is unpronounceable, but I pronounce it, I lick its print, its nervure, the skeleton of what sounds like the repeated call of the unseen bird in the oak.

And "rendezvous," what language was that in? What color? Did it say "rendezvous"? No. As it happens, a mute direction. It "said" the thing in ghost. I did recognize the ever so light and urgent voice of my father, his febrile and confident way of indicating the essential, and also in secret, as if we were at the limit, and since one never knows where that is one is p . . .

this ghost of a voice that whispers from so near, in a pearl grey silk language – for it's a secret – yes that's it, all this is secret, I don't know why, one must not have seen it, heard it, it can only happen if it's as if nothing had happened, one will say nothing, you shall say nothing, you shall say nothing to yourself, swear, I swear, swear to nobody, I swear to nobody, yes but swear again, I swear again

oh yes I swear I swear I swear I sw

In which country?

I feel unwelcome, on the one hand they seem to be expecting me a little, I am expected, I'll have to make some commentaries; on the other hand I hardly know where to put myself it's out in the open, a dug-out room – four meters by three, something like my study but without a roof exposed to the winds to the noise, should there be any, if my friend is there they offer him a seat, but they can't do more, I'm not part of the plan I end up balanced on two chairs, if this upsets me I keep it to myself, in any case it's all a rush, the servants are talking a mile a minute and every minute counts, goes by, whereupon we get up, we go off – whatever I think about this undeniable but dessicated hospitality I keep to myself. – What about lunch? I ask. – What lunch? say our hosts. – All the same, we can't. – We haven't time. – But where I live, we eat, I say. True, I never eat lunch, but my friend hasn't had

anything to eat for . . ., I feel my voice trail off, ring false, –
he is tired, my voice stammers while within me a feeling of
error, of a lack of culture, wells up, here they don't eat that's
how it is, this worries me, a country where no one eats but
I'm the only one who's worried, my friend doesn't say a word,
our hosts hurry us toward the crosswalk over the highway,
the one down-side of this world our hosts warn us, and their
hands tug us toward the edge, this road goes by like mad,
were it not for the wild roar of the motors, the cars go so fast
I wouldn't see a thing

The Hecatomb River you might call it, I say. I feel I'm the
only one bothered by it, the only one who speaks up in any
case. The others, no. I shout! I can't even say *I* shout. But to
see a poor old man, a worker making his way on foot through
this huge flux, and whom a car, invisible because of its speed,
hits, who finds himself on all fours, his cap, which sums up
his whole wretched life, hitting the pavement before him, oh
his threadbare jacket, nobody stops, this wrenches from me
a resounding shout, as if it were me, at that very moment a
young motorcyclist falls, oh horror the car that follows him
already has its enormous black wheel on the black-booted
foot of the motorcyclist, nothing slows it, to slow down is
doubtless an idea as unusual in this world as eating, nobody
"pays attention," payattention seems to me also suddenly like
the manners of another world, the one I come from, that is
the world of which this is the other, I myself as I lean down to
the motorcyclist am on the point of being swept away, what a
place, much later it occurs to me that it is by such differences
of violence that one knows one is in what I call generically the
realm of the dead. However I discover that under the general term are lots of particular places peopled with as many
kinds of dead people as there are kinds of sleep, of dreams, of
forgetting, and delays.

I can tell you I never get used to these harsh places,

14

resigned as they are to an inhumanity that causes a chemical reaction of malaise in me, an atrocious inadequacy, internal misery, I feel my blood boil in my veins, I must have that spinach complexion my mother hates – every time it's a shock, a shriek of exile, yet another invention of anguish, this panic is new, and each time no time, no time, they breathe down my neck, quick hurry up, as if they told me, say your prayers, sign here, settle, pay up and out you go! Go home it's late! late! The word late! sounds like a knell. The welcome is brief indeed. However in the end I get used to these unwonted brutal stays, to their dust the misery in the air, the rough manners with neither pity nor cruelty, their activity regulated by laws of nature such as govern the lives of insects, they cross the highway, they fall over, they die. I keep a journal of these travels. And I confess that the horror I feel, added to the injuries inflicted on my self-esteem, the cares, the feeling of being forever in the wrong, don't keep me from liking to be there. What do I mean by "like"? I've never known. Once I make it through the curtain of horror I have no regrets, not that I feel good, but within me there's a profound acquiescence to some necessity. I admit and I consent: if the other side is only accessible at this price I would not wish to lack the courage to pay. Were I a sort of citizen, a resident of the place . . .

doubtless I would not have this sense of discrepancy, of the spirit's torsion, of spiritual lameness, of disagreement and even of stifling but stifled disapprobation. Oh I disagree, but it's not my job to judge worlds I only visit as a guest.

I understand perfectly that I am privileged, for I meet no other strangers. I am given a visa for the duration, I have no choice, the border crossing, if there is any, if there is one, is behind me, I wasn't present at the transition. This is one of the ways I recognize that I have crossed over: just as one doesn't die, there's no one to ferry you over, one crosses and one has crossed are the same time, as in a dream the present undergoes a scenery change, just as I am transported from one present to another without passage, without any past. But once I am on the other side, what has changed, and which I sense immediately is the thickness of time. There will be very little, my whole body is on the alert, for someone like me the air is rarefied, all the signals in my brain, in my lungs, transmit, as to a diver who dares the dark depths, quick quick-quickquicklivequick, everything starts to rush, and right away this fastforward life is harsh and pure, I go as straight as an angel on a mission, what I think, if I think, comes later, here you live, and that's all. Fire. And no details

"This lovely, crisp, golden Saturday, with a hole in my heart, I had to love it and therefore I loved it, as one loves despite everything the dreadful days-of-ending, when one knows that the end, bringer of separation, is near, days trickling poison whose every drop one wants to suck, chew each crust of the embers. Unlivable but one is happy to live, one wants to feel everything one wants to run away from, lose nothing of the suffering since the whole day has the blood-sweetness of adieu. The taste of ending endowed this Saturday with an incalculable coefficient of grandeur every-one could sense without any of us exchanging a glance. All of us were there for the end of the year. In this case each is contained in the conclusion of his or her own destiny. And He, *hero of the end*, who was nearing the finish line, He coming to his end was present, glorious, royal, naturally, He piloted this day which would take him from us, smiled much as usual, neither more nor less vibrant than Himself. We were all guided by the last star's polar shine. Each time I hear the voice of my mother call my name from the depths, I think the Hour has come, I race toward the end, sure she has fallen, and often it's the Orange Juice. She has set it on the stair. I gulp it down as if it were the last. To die is to fear dying. But He, that Saturday, shone calmly over the hours. All of us, the disciples, knew it was the last time, that you were using, O Socrates, the last of your strength. Surrounded as if by sailors, giving you the grandeur of a captain preparing to go down. Weak and strong, absolute and the whole day sinks overboard. As the day ends he gives me The Biggest Gift, while the throng of disciples takes its leave and filters out. You speak to me of afterwards. 'The only immortals,' he says, I quote, 'are the books that live after us.' This is 'the best *part*,' he says, or maybe '*parle*,' it's hard to hear in the wind. This he affirms, from the depths, and publicly, we shall continue, the books will not be stopped by death, he says, in the day's heavy seas, I guzzle his words, their taste the Orange Juice rainbow in the darkness. They were immensely consoling. I began to be able to bear these last hours, this end is not the end, I was sadly happy. Only the book is big enough to get across the stopped current alive. There we were together for the day's final rays of light, the disciples bid him farewell and leave. I believe this to be the end, I go – at the moment when the Traveler of the end is about to see the sail, which is no longer far, He has his face turned toward the horizon while I am watching the invisible coming to be reflected in the eyes of the one concerned. And that's when those eyes, in which I would not wish to see that which does not regard me, and as I am turning toward the exit, that's when they look down at me. He tells me: 'I'm taking the train tomorrow. And of course you'll find me at Athens Station at 5:30 p.m.' I was dazzled. I wasn't expecting the station. And anxious, for I am thinking I have a class – *j'ai cours*, I think – at that time. My whole soul stammers, astonished, the word *cours* slips away from me, grows enigmatic, is it *cour, court, cours, cours* – is it courtyard, brief, class, run?

I'm not sure I still have a class, not sure where I am, where I will be. So this is the vertigo my mother has when she no longer knows, at the supermarket, if she still has class, and if so where, for the river is no longer in its bed. And it's me whom the famous moment-of-death deprives of its means? How much surer of his footing the One-who-goes-off is than the-one-who-remains. Needless to say I hide the wretched whirlwind of my rout. When Annie my beloved friend went off last month, it was she who guided me, the pit was bottomless, she told me about a beautiful flat stone on which I could put my foot, and I let myself be guided by her. In my mind I turned over this unexpected one-more-moment I'd never have thought possible. How limited the imagination is. 'Go with him to the last train' had just taken the place of the last hour, now put off to the station, and never had I felt so poor in spirit so dried up, so lacking in great and admirable ideas, so ill served by memory, vain regrets needled me, I haven't prepared for the exam, nothing comes to mind, ah if only I could reread Plato, Montaigne, here we are, a reprieve is granted me, I mean Him, a day is rendered deific, and in advance unforgettable, and there I am thwarted by the advent of a delay which fills me on the one hand with archangelic bliss, on the other hand and at the same time with the inertia that prefigures death. It's as if from the prison of a dream he'd told me: something might be done about the death sentence. But I need a Computer. And in the cell of the dream this would be said in veiled tones of reproach: fate could be outsmarted on one condition, but this is precisely the one condition I could not be counted on to fulfill. I admit that nothing in our entire lives has come between us, except the Computer. The Computer, and its threatening French name: the *Ordinateur*. The Ordinator. It's as if, this time, I saw the Sail or the Veil that my whole life I've been unable to face, the place on the map of the worlds where power meets its impotence. A trifle checkmates everything: everywhere in literature this can be seen, it's a poplar leaf, it's a minute's lateness, it's a lost address, it's a phone number no longer in service, I know them all except for the Computer. Send me to Peru to find the antidote, I'll do it. *You see*, he thinks. No surprise, indignation, or hope in his thoughts. But, I murmur, *there is* a Computer. This is neither a fiction, nor a twitch in the dream. It was alwaysalready there, sitting on my desk like the sculpture of a dog that has never worked. I don't deny I've never turned it on. But around its neck it wears one of those sheets of paper consecrated by my mother's handwriting, a sheet upon which she has inked in big red letters: 'you must plug it in and push power (on the right).' I pushed Power.

So I thought I'll see him *one more last time*. Already I fear and tremble: what will it be like? Now we hug goodbye but this is the 'this-is-not-the-last-time' farewell, there's a sweet reprieving strangeness. Tomorrow a few more minutes. And *after*, the books will never be apart and will be immortal. For now we are restored. Everyone has left. In the next interval of time I wonder how to get home, for it is late, it will be too dark, I'll lose my way. I consider leaving my car in Sounion parking lot where I left it this morning. But if I go home without my car, I'll have to come back for it tomorrow, to go to the station. I ponder. Already seven o'clock. At this point I notice that daylight has stopped fading. It is not getting darker. It is still bright. So nothing stops me fetching my car from the lot. Time is on hold. I've alreadyseen that in the Bible. I springintoaction. I look for my keys. I findthemquick. The keys are my mother's. No problem opening. Nothing resists. I goquick home in my car

I'll read Plato. I'll read the whole time Socrates would have had to spend in prison between the end and the last time. And tomorrow I'll see Him at the station, in life. I saw all that, while I was at the wheel, I was driving and I saw myself again watching him depart on this lovely golden Saturday with a hole in my heart, I saw myself tomorrow, at the station,"

I wrote all that on one of those pads of paper my mother stocked up on last year, she bought two years' worth I told myself thinking "mama fancies she's leaving me what I need to live on *after*," I said: "this is quite a stack of notebooks" to push the paper sail secretly away, and my mother said: "they were on sale, half-price." So, as usual, I thought I saw night coming too fast. Later on, I wrote, we'll be immortal. I felt a kind of sadness loom. But for now, everything is here, I wrote, it won't get dark

"*Demeurathène?* my mother repeats, where did you say? in the drawer?" And I repeat: "Demeurathène, on the shelf."

"Two Meurathènes?" cries my mother, and in vain I repeat, Danaides of the telephone that we are, I pour, she pours, in vain and vice versa, because of the meddling of the Invisibles different but no less discreet than the Teleerinyes that yesterday crossed the paths of Proust's and Kafka's sorrows and a hundred years later here they are still making my mother and me sound like buffoons. – Listen oh listen I called. – Du Mourathène? cries my mother. Deux meurathène? My mother's voice echoes my voice

– Could you, I say and I pitch my voice north toward her again, find me *Demeure, Athènes*, it's on the shelf to the left of the table, I say, it's lying down, black and white.

– I thought it was some sort of medicine.

Well, it is a drug, I tell myself, and tender-eared my mother detected my need of a remedy. I who thought my anxiety was hidden by the telephonic distance. You see how the subject can get out of the speaker's control.

20

Change of itinerary. More and more I travel in the realm of the dead, less and less in the vigilant world, that is, the world that keeps vigil for the world to come and which I recognize as a vigil in that my mother rises later and later. This is how Absence moves in, I tell myself, on transparent feet into daily life, it depopulates the mornings, it drapes its silences over the house until morning is done. But I also move to counter it. I exorcize it, I conjure it, I see it everywhere it isn't, such is its strength, to be what it is not gives it an edge, maybe even when it's not there, when the void is calm, when the present sits on the stairs, I am already imagining It rustling its ocean nearby, I observe the world from the standpoint of the catastrophe, I will be sitting on the platform with no mama no station no bus, in my mind I won't see her white Manchester hat waving from the street corner, the City will be muffled by the cloth of Oblivion, I will no longer be thinking about the oilcloth that today serves her as a forever fresh metonymy linking the table of the Oran Paradise Beach to the table in Paris I will be sitting with no past on the wharf next won't come time will be standing still. Fearing it so continuously, I no longer know whether I arm myself against it or whether I summon it. I can't not feel it leaning against the doors, housing its dark thoughts in the cupboards, on the coat hooks everywhere it hangs its imitations of my mother. And until the kitchen orchestra, under the direction of my mother, wakes with a din around noon I keep my mind in the enchanted places of books. It's as if I took a dose of Demeurathène, strangest of drugs, a book that gives the illness and the cure for the illness in a single dose. Am I ill? I can't stand the paths that plunge into the gorges of forests, *seem* to plunge, says my brother, I only like coming back, and even then I want the paths to come out on broad bays. The broken branch that lets its arms fall from the shoulder of the oak hurts me. Wednesday morning I said to my brother: old Raffia, we'll keep her, thinking: Raffia the old chair, once my mother's pride and joy, her avant-garde find in the Grandes Galeries de Paris, the first conquest of a young provincial from the north of Germany, in her daring sprint to be first in the heart of Europe, in 1935 already, taking Paris first, by The Chair. A nimble chair in sycamore for the timbers, and for the body that daring esparto grass of exotic weave that the young Ève asked the vendor for in 1935, as she would ask again later, in 2005, if the thing would hold, with her Germanic confidence in the word of a department store clerk. It was a chair with a future. The chair of the future, says my mother. We'll keep it I say. That Raffia, says my brother. I could put it in my study I was thinking. Later. A chair full of my mother's pride. When the fashion was for dark I already liked what was light says my mother, I went to the Galeries, first I spotted a white Moroccan rug with black designs in the corners, suddenly what's this I see? Chairs nobody would buy. Wood untreated, a movable back of straw-colored raffia. Will they last? I asked the clerk. He says yes. He had no idea what he was talking about. I bought the chairs, which have not let me down

"We'll keep it," I told my brother. I didn't say: "we'll keep it forever," as soon as I heard the future tapping at the pane I fastened the windows, there's a time for the present and for what comes next and it's not time yet. We'll keep Raffia, the last of them, the others didn't survive my mother's moves, Raffia's the only French one. Perhaps her peers live on in Algeria, along with Omi's German buffet, we will never know. Right away I thought: let's not think. And before dusk – Come see this! my brother shouted. That same Wednesday. There was my brother standing in front of Raffia, crushed. I'd sat down and as if it heard me say "I'll keep it," and as if *One* wanted to send me a warning, as in Homer one sees Fate signaling in vain to mortals by definition full of disbelief, it fell to pieces in a second changing its form from that of quad-

22

ruped to that of dust. My brother is innocent. He who never sits on Raffia, he who lays his clothes on the seat, for the back tilts, that he should on that day have sat down, my remark is the cause. It must have switched on some kind of affection, a gesture of hospitality, the very idea of treating it like a chair, something One hadn't done for years – so we hadn't realized that for a long time it had been a mere appearance. The collapse was brutal. Dead as a badly killed beast. A large splinter of bone wrenched from the left shoulder exposing the big chrome screw. Legs disjointed, pelvis cracked, I went out. The last act is naturally my brother's department. As a doctor, as heir to our doctor father, the master of anatomy. What's more he is the only one in the family who has the power to care for the bodies that have just breathed their last with the neutral, economical, affect-less gestures that spare the feelings of the now defenseless body. For even if the soul no longer resides there, a trace of suffering adheres to the body. Or maybe it was waiting for this moment to go away, I tell myself. Raffia. She was tired. Maybe she wanted to end as a chair, I tell myself. But I keep my animism to myself. Everything is sign, I myself am signed, signatory. I don't agree. If I had four feet and a raffia back, I'd collapse myself. Whereas my brother is innocent. The proof is the way he concludes the chair story. Three quick blows and the feet are kindling. Raffia in the trash. Next time we make a fire says my brother. Scrolls of sycamore.

"Did you tell mama?" I ask and as suspected he says: "No." This without counting on dreams. I've alreadylived that. In vain do we wish to make off with the dead. Here comes my mother, alerted by the noise. Her deafness adds a threatening din. – Who threw this out on me? she roars. I repair everything! – Alas, I say, there is the irreparable. Want to see? She wants to make off with it, I sense. So off we fly, never mind the cane and the slowness. I hear her hear the chair, my

23

mother, as fastslowly we descend the stairs, my mother's soul stretched out beating the air with its old wings, nose honed. "You shall outlive me . . ."

I've alreadylived that.

– You will outlive me, you said, said The Chair. *Nil opis, nobis tua vota tulerunt.* Your wishes were no use to me. I believe I hear the chair. You and your optimism. At which point she says the dreadful word: *occidimus.* We are dead. She means: I am dead. But she extends her death to everything that touches her, her shadow, her pain, my mother's entire history, the joyous betrothal begun in Paris in 1935 and brutally terminated an hour ago. Two notes regret and resentment, they affect mama, she who repairs everything but the irreparable. I show my mother a worm-eaten leg. The worms invisible. Only the hundreds of holes. Their minuscule size paints the infinite perfidy of the act. The chair has fallen under a thousand blows.

– It is noon. Good night, says my mother. What's done is done.

I have the feeling that my beloved feels, remotely, that she is in a scene in which Ève the survivor is unaware of acting, it's the Cemetery, I mean the Cemetery-Scene, or the Scene-of-the-Cemetery, that posthumous sequence to which all poets make a pilgrimage, for here the literary revolt gets decided and countersigned, here, on the lips of a skull, one drinks the poison of survival, from the way her arm trembles on my arm I feel that she too, like Shakespeare, like Balzac, Stendhal, Aeschylus, Proust, Freud, Derrida, sees herself hurrying to speak one last time to a cadaver who only yesterday told her: one of us will outlive the other, hurrying with the freedom of folly toward this body, like Montaigne, not daring to admit that one's secret intention is to refute utterly any pretension reality might claim to laying down the law, defying the sentence with a superhuman sprint, standing up to

24

authority, the feeble nature of Nature, and to walk roughshod over God. My mother looks at the thousand toothmarks. That's how it'll be, she's thinking. "The worms are hungry," she says. Impossible to know whether the sentence is aimed at the worms whose voracity she reproaches. Or if she's simply noting a natural process. For the moment, the voice is unreadable. I put the devoured leg back down. – Do you want to keep the raffia? I ask. – I've never seen the raffia without the chair, says my mother. I don't want to keep it, but I want to look at it at least. The chair's raffia back is rolled up in the bin for dry trash. Let me see it. I unroll it. Life has truly forsaken it. It has become inanimate. To think it has borne me on its back thousands of times. In any case says my mother, it's done for. It's finished: it's finished.

I went upstairs to write. What am I doing putting paper and ashes on my head? My brother whistles to me. He calls my spirits back to the world of reality. I see the fulminations of his big yellow pullover. Therefore I am beside him. Whistling is between us. No words. I put my arms around the bulky yellow pullover. You need long arms. It reminds me of the extensions Vautrin needed for his arms, to get them around Vauquier's waist. The feeling of bulk does me good. After the moment of stripping to the bone. I'm writing a hymn to my brother, I say. And I am going to buy some veal, calf's liver, says my brother. I'd better do the shopping without mama. At noon there are too many people. Big yellow bird goes off. *Vau . . . veau . . . vautour* – Vulture, says the writing. It is sitting in the south-east corner of my study on the ghost of Raffia.

I am not sick. I see everything. I hear everything. I shift twenty centimeters, the width of a thought: I see myself seeeverything, heareverything.

The difference with my brother is only this twenty-centimeter gap. The way he receives the letters I don't

25

write, it's like knowing when one must whistle, not the words, the song, it's a secret that began in the old days on the beaches where before we learned to read French words we read Homer, what He had written in the sand and on the rocks, with his feet. Everything I do not tell him, we go on "a sacred promenade" I was thinking, I don't tell him – and after a few hundred meters, it has all been translated into his inner journal. I don't know exactly which veins, pores, palms, what physical system it goes through, but this is a fact. The proof that the sacred is stronger than anything is my brother doesn't believe in it, only half of us believe in it, which is me, and despite the skepticism, indifference, or perhaps thanks to indifference, distraction, inattention, every single thing I want to pass along to him without telling him reaches him. Or almost.

The Squirrel too, I gave no explanation, it was totally impossible. Even today four years have passed without my being able to approach the Squirrel with my voice. I couldn't tell my brother: picture Abraham's breast the morning he finds his ass stretched out lifeless. And he, Abraham, imagine, he feels like the ass is being torn from his breast. He feels he has the ass in his body, in his belly, in his whole life. And he sees the ass on the ground, lying on the dryish grass. It isn't sleeping. Lying on its side, felled. The first time – that it doesn't come. He adores it oh how he adores it, you can't say this, it has no name, it doesn't exist in reality, it is carved into the suffering he now has where his breast used to be. Lifeless are the words with which he strikes his brow. Because the other word he doesn't say, it is a word he won't ever receive on his tongue. He sits or falls down, he doesn't have his yesterday head, in a flash he has fallen into the huge cavity of today's torture. His breast has swelled up to make room for the big hole. And in this jagged basin sobs bubble up. O, o, o, o, o. One can't not weep when one hears this cry, me at least, this *cry of despair*, this lamentation that calls God by only *one* note of his name, for there'll be no response, each time I hear it, I weep, this is the cry weeping in the moan of Hamlet's *Ghost*, the same cry, there's only one despair, this is Alcyone's cry which, even when it is in verse and in paper, makes me weep. And right this moment, as I paint Abraham's animal cry of pain, tears fall.

For better or for worse at this hour Abraham is alone therefore he is with his ass. Later on he'll be grateful his ass lay down daintily that night, so that his father Abraham, his brother, son Abraham might find him easily, already gone but still there, find him before the others, so the two of them have this time to themselves. A moment when Abraham can shout and weep over the ass. Obviously. The whole of the life is there, stretched out, such a well-earned long tough life, not just the life, but a life-saved, a life-but-for-death, so many times, and this is their life, the life that the ass, only the ass, gave to Abraham, that he gave back to him every single day re-transcribed on the spot, living it with him. Sharing with him the bread and the terrors.

"Lucky for me you're here," each time Abraham was in difficulty, he took care to say this to the ass, for so it was, the ass was always if not the whole of Abraham's strength at least an incalculable part of that more than abrahamic strength, for no one can surpass his own strength without the help of another's strength yoking itself silently to the great team. And even at this moment "What would I do without you?" he was saying. The Witness lies sleeping on his left side. And Abraham tells himself that even now the ass bears witness, as usual, to what is beyond him. Him. "Do you sleep, my love? Sleep," Abraham can't *say* that, but that doesn't matter, he thinks it and he knows that the ass hears, that's what ears are for. Lucky you're there, they think. Imagine the idea that comes to him all of a sudden. It's not an intellectual "idea," it's an impulse of his whole being. He puts his hand on the ass, first it's a kind of shyness, on his shoulder, with uncertainty, uncertain. It's that he doesn't know. Since this time he is not sure of his witness's approval. But a second later he has put his hand on his shoulder. And the skin is warm, as usual. An unexpected feeling of contentment causes Abraham to tremble. Not that the ass is given back to him but that he still has him, he's not taken from him, he doesn't know for how long, but there's some time, between the sleeping and the end. Right away I touch him, the clairvoyant eyes of the blind come to me, I spell him, I've put my lips on his upper lip. I run my hand over his entire body, over his belly where my fingers trace the seams incised in the fur by the straps, I comb, I touch, I smooth, Abraham murmurs, as if he were his own witness, not a centimeter of this being that my whole hunger to touch won't have touched, to print every detail of the animal of my life in my inner book. Imagine him using his fingertips as his lips, his lips as his eyes, his eyes as his tongue. One has an archaic, childlike fear of overlooking a centimeter which would then be missing from the whole henceforth preserved in the temple of the soul. So he goes over every inch of the animal, with the utmost care. He will, at a moment that cannot be precisely determined, have thought to snip a lock of hair. This comes later, not long before the adieu. He cuts awkwardly, quite high, quite far from the skin, for he finds he's overdoing things with these old-wife practices. But he's afraid, if he doesn't, he'll regret it later, hence too late, and so there he is sad, humbly cutting, the hair resists, the knife doesn't catch, finally he has a pinch of fine pink and brown hair in his hand a wisp he wraps in a white handkerchief. Because of the handkerchief, his thoughts turn to the tallith – but this can only be a thought. A tallith big enough for an ass, only a dream can come up with that.

Whereas for the squirrel, it wouldn't have been impossible, but – and it's a miracle – all I said to my brother: bury it – a miracle that I could put into this single word *bury* such urgent pleading. BURY IT. As if I touched my brother's knees and chin. I couldn't say: don't kill this dead thing. Do not consign this unfortunate creature to the Trash. Do not throw the mortal remains, which you tell me are magnificent, of one of the protective divinities that haunt the woods of my texts, into the trash with the household garbage, the oyster shells, rejects without an afterlife. I made no comment upon the figure of the Squirrel, everywhere living in my books, ever since Squirrel The First, the half-squirrel, whose spirit haunts *Tomb* (where I laid it) or rather over which *Tomb*, the book, has kept watch, as you prefer, for decades. How everything began to transform itself starting with and because of a Squirrel in Washington Square, my life in an instant turning into literature, without my being aware of it, that October morning in 1964. I thought it dead. Right afterwards, a bound . . . resurrection. Then from death to resurrection, from book to book, from literature into reality, I have never inaugurated a notebook without a wave from one squirrel to another, and so on. Later it turns up in the shape of Goya's half-dog. Forever more alive than dead or rather: rather than dead forever still living. But one day, when my brother calls me on the phone, telling me: "Sit down," I realize that, this time, "it" is really dead. My brother found it dead on my bed. When I beg my brother: Bury it, he doesn't say no.

– Swear, swear I say, swear. I should stop there. And for the first time it was done.

– Sit down, says the voice of my brother, meaning: "so you don't fall down." I've never spoken of the Squirrel to him. He has never read *Tomb*. Had he read it, this would not have unlocked the secret. Not even I knew the underground geography of the Squirrel kingdom. All of a sudden, when the voice of my brother the cantor rang out on the phone, I was gripped by a heartrending, luminous emotion, such as the sound of the shofar will awake in the hearts when its bellowing comes to tell the loving what they have failed to believe so long as it was not too late. Once I sat down, I listened to my brother painting the ruins. Picture the sack of the apartment of the Rue Morgue, the furniture upside down, picture the typhoon in *Moby Dick*. The walls still stand, bearing witness to something with no proper name: what thieves, what winds, what madness, what powers of destruction, what demons have received what order, what terrifying need wanted not just to throw hundreds of books into space, but to rip them apart, tear out eyes, tongues, lacerate posters, photographs, wallpaper, slash sheets to rags. I listened to the cantor enumerate the destruction that harrowed his voice. My brother wandered through the rubble and there was no author. All the fury was within. From the outside the house looks like a sleeper, impossible to guess that inside is the siege and extermination of Troy. Nothing remains of my private city but unsigned ravage. – Beethoven too? I murmured. – Torn to shreds. Too. The gods didn't protect us, they are shattered. – They didn't open the drawers, says my brother. And in conclusion all they were after was your writing. I wish I understood. I pictured the catastrophe, softened by the voice of my brother, from afar I glimpsed an end of the world that he tried to lessen, above all don't throw anything out, I pleaded, nobody knows what lives live in those old bones. What's more every ten minutes I got the description of the next misfortune, and blessed the messenger for the continued fidelity of the funereal phone. I held back my tears, as one does when one doesn't yet know the extent of the disaster.

And that was the Squirrel. Believe it or not, but believe my brother. The author was him. The Squirrel.

For four years I haven't been able to end this tale.

Four years ago I said: Bury it.

I said: Swear. I said: Did you do it? – How can I? Swear! Swear. – It's as good as done. – Swear! groaned my voice. – I swear. Ok, I'm going now. – Come back – I'm going. – How shall I? – Find a pine tree. You'll tell me –

He told me. I stop here.

May I never be able to tell The End.

– You are so vulnerable! says my brother. I am a trifle subject to these violent emotions. I take things naturally hard, says my brother

While I carry within me the ravages of the Squirrel, my brother buries.

I had so many dead to weep over, for whom there are too few tears.

You never know whom you are burying. Go gently, I was saying. I thought: religiously, but I had to be content with thinking about my religious necessity religiously. You can't say this to the brother who does the burying. Still, burying to please me counts as an act in the invisible religion. Among my revenants the Squirrel is the most literarily revenant, the most literary of my revenants. I could hardly tell my brother, there you bury my most ancient god, my religion, the most forsaken of my prophets, last of the Mohicans, Incarnation of Literature's Genius, Fate's Gambler, outwitter of verdicts, in that little hole you bury several continents and four tombs, it's The City you bury, Comeback City, first and the last cradle, you bury the adorable error of the truth, from this day forth there will be no more Resurrections in Reality henceforth they resuscitate in the dream world.

Later, when a year has gone by, one day I'll be out walking with my brother in the place in my being where I once had my poet friend by my side, when the ancient rhythm of walking makes the flood of my inner book's emotions well up, as I'm thinking very hard about The Squirrel, and then of the immense Squirrel corpus, I'll want to tell him the beginning.

31

One fine morning in October 1964, death was starting up again, one is out walking alive, out of the blue, death turns up, Washington Square cemetery, "submission to the inner reality" my friend said, he was smiling at the idea of the end, I staggered, seeing the cadaver of a squirrel half-buried in the ground, as if it had hurried to hide its death in Hell but, taken by surprise as it was going down, it remained stuck there like an inhabitant of Herculaneum "this is the secret of art" my friend the American poet said, I staggered, seeing in the cadaver's half-body the annunciation of the fate of my poet friend. I saw two dead. I know, I fear it in vain, ever since Washington Square, I live on the dead. "Submission to the door of the book" says my friend. "Pass death, and there's literature. Descend underground, follow the squirrel, it will take you to the root of the secrets." So there are gods with short lives, I tell myself, for Homer the gods come into our beds with the grace of the young things in novels, in Manhattan Hector is a squirrel, or maybe it was Fabrice. In those days, I'll tell my brother, I worshipped the friend and the squirrel with the same terror. I saw life I saw death. I saw life: I saw death. That's all I have to say.

HENBANE

Are the terror and pain I read about in my book the book's invention, does my book lay it on too thick, turn itself into something orgiastic, and why, what malevolent spirit roams its domains? What sorcerer most unlike myself, and feeding nonetheless on my disorder, pouncing on all the shadows and shudders that slip in among my souls? Truly, it's a struggle. Never have the three levels of my desk been such a mess, so buried under landslides of books torn out of their covers the hundreds of notebooks one devouring the next like mad horses turning on each other in the streets of Rome their savage furies roused by the crazy pressure of the coming massacres. Suicide before assassination is the scene on my desk. I lay out a perfectly healthy sheet of paper, without the least sign of derangement, two-thirds filled with lines written in my usual firm hand, an instant later it's gone, no, not even, it's as if I had tossed the paper as a sacrifice at the maw of a hydra all the more terrifying as it is materially hidden from me, I don't know where it is, it is everywhere, its word agape and smearing its everlasting hydra shriek over the whole room, I inhabit a maw whose boundaries are hidden from me, everything I cook up, create, is promptly seized, against my will I grow the monster that shapes within me, or maybe on me, this paunch of death. It immediately turns my every effort to undo it to its own advantage. At dawn, colorless hope already breathing, I set things in order. Less than an hour later the tidal wave of derangement comes along. Twenty striding pages come tumbling down making such a tangle there's no point trying to set them to rights again. Might as well put them out of their misery. With a pencil I nudge them toward the bin, they are not yet dead, but who cares, they are contaminated, their poison leaks out, I know. Between believing doing make believing wanting not to believe the unbelievable believable error is changed into terror of verity

I am afraid of mama dying, that's the truth that's the error. I think first. First I think I'm scared, I'm scared of thinking, I'm scared of the thought, I'm scared it thinks before I do that it thinks too fast much too so much that it gallops off with me it thinks without my authorization without my consent that it counter-thinks what I, furthermore, don't in the least think. I know a lot about thought's tricks. It runs away with me, without my heart, my language, it is pythic, it has numerous uncontrollable, contradictory properties like the thermometer's mercurial worm if ever it break out of its tube. It leaps twisting and turning, betrayal is its essence. Which is why it provokes and fascinates.

First I think I am afraid that mama – next I write: I get a grip on the fear that won't let go of me, I want at least to pin it down, not be afraid to look it in the face, challenge it, interrogate it, spell out its name. Yes, I write, I clamp the words between my fingers between my teeth, I don't yield to their jerks and twists. I nail down: "*I am afraid of mama dying, that's the truth, that's the error.*" This fixes the worm that bores into my brain. Now I face the worm, without blinking. This is not the same thing as being asleep, I tell myself. In my orchard, for instance, after lunch for a nap, like my father, my brother, my fiancé, King Hamlet, all those, ears open to the poison, who trust their siesta in the orchard. I don't sleep, not me. I see the worm. It's a phial slim as a sentence or on the contrary filled to the soul with the damned juice of jusquiame, *henbane*. And into the porches of my ears I see something pour the leprous liqueur extract of *Hyoscyamus niger* viscous bristling with glandular hairs with big soft stem-less leaves huge teeth that grows in the rubble naturally and which even the handbooks of naturalists, as if seized by repulsion, hesitate to picture, unless the scientists have themselves been contaminated by the perversity of the dread plant and, surreptitiously fail to alert the visitor. I see the treacherous creature that pours the liqueur everybody from Shakespeare, or even Marlowe already, knows has such antipathy for our blood, it is designed to betray thus to make evil pass for good as quick as quicksilver which, in the name of all that quickens, brings death all the faster all the more inevitably, and this creature that knows all the body's ways to kill me right to where the soul is, is me. It was me.

And when no one will believe that I can with a sentence, a thought, a mental invention turned into a totally imaginary tale, poison myself, be about to abuse the whole ear of Denmark, mama will believe me. Otherwise I'd be dead, I will at this very moment die from my self-inflicted injection of a phrase grown up out of my ruins and horribly toxic.

May to September season of blooms, yellow flowers veined with brownish-purple. But at this very moment, three lines and three seconds below, the noise-mama gets up, frttfftte, tender antidote, frttffrtt, frttffrtte of mama's slippppersss quick, irregular, rushed, it drives into the staircase the vermin that make cracks in the vile scaly skin of the heart, and life starts up again in my scabby blood. Maybe I'm only subject and condemned to these death crises because during the summer months my mother is just close enough for my wretched inner character to venture too far? Maybe with mama close enough to be under my senses every hour of the day when she comes out of absence (that is from the tenth to the nineteenth hour of the day), I see, hear, touch, smell all the states of my mother's body and hence my awareness of the work that ruins her never sleeps? And so by my own hand I am robbed of life, of crown, of queen, and ghost-infested until ten o'clock each and every morning. Ten! I say.

Then flies buzz at the windows, nothing seems to keep them from the kingdom of the air, they fling themselves in vain against the diaphanous glass and fall back down.

This book will herein call itself: Jusquiame, or Henbane.

How can I not give in to the violent charms of the word, of the thing – of the name? Is it not a lovely name? I ask myself. What a lovely face, a lovely figure, for a plague. Stramonium, belladonna the beautiful damned, adorable parent, incestuous sister of sleep, what a family! Venerable venomous. Mama is not awake.

PUT ME A GHOST AT THE
EMBARCADERO

Is everything OK?

On and on down the road with my brother beside me, my brother with his sister at his side on the other side his cane, the same road at the end of it there's brush and burning brambles this doesn't mean there is nothing beyond, one can even, off in the depths of the painting, above the forest, glimpse the edge of the sea again, at least my brother can for being taller than I am he sees what I don't see, always the same road which is never the same, down the same not the same go our footsteps, our somewhat out-of-tune footsteps, faster, I think; the whole body of my brother thinks: slow down, a single story containing two stories, at the same moment or within a few centimeters of one another, one of the two thinks: death, one: life, my right arm under my brother's left arm, the man out walking with his dog growing bigger as he comes toward us from the east can't know who these two people are, the man thinks the husband the dog thinks the brother, nor can one know who writes what first and what next, next and

37

consequently I don't know which of the stories goes a little faster because sometimes that's the one that slows down a little, if you ask me I think only death but mama on the other hand is more full of life, so that I never know exactly what the weather is like today if I do life if I do death, the one comes along on the heels of the other, hence they join and color one another, yet another question I say with two answers, everything's OK, I say, everything marches straight toward the east without end, I stumble but not too much because of my brother's arm, the cane on his side, I try the cane but it trips me up, the pen is my cane, it's always with me, on me, in me, otherwise I would fall, with my cane hooked to my heart my brother on the other side I wend my way and I regret everything, everything I love that I have loved, I regret each year each friend woman man minute I regret every step of the way, my brother and all the brothers he brings along with him, all the brothers he is that he hides, represents, I regret the road, the writing, I regret everything that is and therefore is not everything that is not, whereas my brother says: I've been happy. Then I regret terribly the book that will not have been written, I will die, and I will regret dying with it, it is "over there" I say, everything that is and is not I can however tell my brother, on my right side, whatever one can't tell I can tell my brother as we go as far we can, right to the brushwood. Beyond the brush is the Embarcadero. I haven't the courage to push past the wall of thorns. Had I the courage, I could unfold a tale each act of it more monumental than the last scene, each word of it rippling with light like a firefly, its secrets having the power to wake the sleeping imagination of the world with a start. But I have no idea where to find such courage, nor what it is made of.

– Thereupon one would see that the Leytter comes to the Embarcadero, and throws itself into the sea. – Oh, if only I could be a Leytter. But I need an Ovid to turn me into a little river. Already I'm doing something I'm not allowed to do without getting my fingers singed, it isn't forbidden, but it requires great attention every second, mama's skin is a lot more fragile than you think, I say. I tremble violently when I force myself to get right up close to her secret. Not that she's hiding herself, but she's not showing herself either. Each time you touch her you're in danger of hurting her. I hurt mama yesterday when I grazed her forearm with my wristwatch I tell my brother. I don't conceal this. I announce it. It's bad news. The illness is growing worse. We have to follow it. I tell my brother this the better to tell myself. One should announce it to oneself on the radio. I blame myself. To kiss my mother I now have to tilt my face toward a patch of intact skin, set my lips half a millimeter from her hand, graze a finger, or the lobe of her ear or the tip of her nose, taking care not to touch her with my hands. It crosses my mind that the surface of unaffected skin, incalculably shrinking as it is – perhaps each minute-of-my-mother is a minute of happiness, perhaps all the terror out of which the rest of my life is cut is a kind of happiness since it abundantly nourishes the furnace of regret. I never sleep. Yesterday I scratched mama with my wristwatch, after that I burned the thumb on my right hand. Still, this doesn't keep me from writing, not yet.

The danger is falling asleep, getting thrown off track – while the enemy tunnels under our lives with the help of our negligence, the lichen of ill will – I mean drawing the wool over one's eyes, putting up with the presence of evil just as one goes along with a dubious government, lying a little to oneself that this pemphigoid is now part of the family, we look after it, we coddle it, soon we'll have grown complacent about its tricks. I have to accuse myself.

I barely kiss her, that very second the little ring of leather cut her skin, a ten-centimeter wound: I confess. Here a bandage, there a bandage: Mama's limbs are papered with ever-shifting bandages. The wounds open and close successively like a hibiscus in bloom. I no longer notice the brownish bruises. They have me tamed. I no longer fear them, I no longer hate them. At ease, with my collusion they hasten to spread their nets of death.

"Hamlet's father, I say, doyouremember, I mean his ghost, Hamlet the ghost," I say. We've reached the bend in the road, in the distance I could see the brushwood porch, my mother always says "there's a limit," that's her law, I was thinking, there's a limit beyond which you don't go, she says, what do you want to prove? "I respect the limit" she says, I was thinking, I could see what was far-off coming closer, the epidermus of the limit dwindling, "where is my limit?" I ask myself, perhaps that's my limit, I tell myself, the skin of my mother, the absolute and limited protection the more and more fragile powerful protection, and beyond the thorn bushes, I might, if I could, no doubt expect to see my father's being waiting for me on the wharf, I imagine the wharf, the place of disembarkation, that is The Embarcadero for those of us who come from the land and I see him clearly – from afar as from close up, sitting on the bollard of the quay in the light-colored suit he used to wear during the war. The difference between my father and mama I tell myself suddenly is no longer as clear cut as before, now that it is getting less and less possible to touch mama, and this thought strikes me painfully, as if a blow from a wristwatch had scraped my soul. But *already I imagine the wharf.* I'm getting ahead of myself, just as one always sees Homer's characters get ahead of themselves for in those days they were all anticipators, pushers and shovers and rebels against limits, and the sorts of frauds of whom my mother totally disapproves. "What's wrong?" *Already* I see him see me running up to him, transported by this divided joy that floods me in such exceptional cases, I never forget that time is counted differently for the dead who return to walk this land, counted differently than for the locals. I alreadysee myself in front of him, I bend to put my lips on his lips, each time I do this – how long are you here for? I ask each time – till this evening, he says. – I'll go tell mama, I'll be right back, I say. For it's always the same. Whenever my dearly departed comes, I must pay my debt for coming back, yes I'm the one who comes back, all I have in the world is this one wish, return as quickly as I can to the knees of my ghost and not leave him again till time is up. All this leaning on my brother's arm I mean on my right arm. – Did you see this carpet of blue flowers? –Those are thistles I say. We are approaching the fiery porch.

Already I'm back with my brother. It's the goddess Metonymy that links me to everything that is attached to me

– Hamlet's father, I say, you know? – A ghost, says my brother, I know. – Hamlet the spirit I say. – He was papa's age. But not at all the same character. Do you believe some places are damned? – I believe some places are holy, I say. – So? – Here. – Have you seen Hamlet? – It's a montage, I say. Given an embarcadero, one is bound to attract ghosts. Take this quay here. And I see him return again. All he wants is to talk to Hamlet and he just can't. It's terrible. In the first moments he starts painting the infernal beauty of a secret, he has a secret, in which he vegetates, when he touches it he burns himself, the cell is papered with fiery thistles, and he – he burns for his secret, he's in love with it, and deprived of it, the secret is the tomb in which he lives, I tell my brother, and everything is metaphor, you mustn't tell, are we in it, are we outside it, he won't write this inner book, he will always be there like the living like the dead, it hurts, it is a tomb speaking, a tomb that groans and weeps and pretty soon it's going to stop, like the shadow of a sheep at the bark of a rooster he returns under the earth. He has just time to chant his misfortune. I come to tell you something I will not tell. The lightning bolt, the revolution, the crime, the truth, if only the world knew, no one will ever know, the world is asleep, my night is without sleep, my fate is to walk, *I walk the night*, night makes me walk, I walk it, there's no walking, when I think I go up I go down, behind and ahead I hear night howl: don't tell! You must not tell. Under my helmet my head is splitting. You must not tell, I won't be able to, you must not say that it must not be told, it's not me, it's the law, the eternal bugle rends my ears, I cry *O i o o o!* Oh horrible Oh help! You have no idea the din in the head of a ghost. I come to swear I will not tell.

– And so? says my brother.

– At that moment, in the very breath in which he says: "sshht, not a word" – he tells. The law wants him to say nothing. *He tells everything.* He tells the Law. And, within the Law, he tells. At the same time, at that very moment.

– Maybe that's how ghosts are. Had you thought of that?

Would that I were a ghost! Already I see myself. I'll forget the law when I say it, I won't write the book I'm writing, I'll write the book I don't write.

– I'll never ever be able to do it, I say to myself, and yet I got an early start

In January 2006 I began saying I would not take any more long trips. First of all I put this forward as a hypothesis. Then more and more clearly. But before that, in December 2005, in the yellow notebook called *Ève and Éri Take Paris*, I jotted: "I've begun to *think* that *soon* I won't take any more long trips." This was a shift of sorts – backwards or forwards? – compared to the year 2004. At that time I couldn't imagine thinking of saying one day I wouldn't take any more long trips, one of these days, without nervously pushing away a state of mind that right away I judged ominous, maleficent, disastrous and as deserving of punishment as bringers of bad news know themselves to be. Except that the messenger I wished to trounce was myself. In 2004 I forbade myself to think I wouldn't take any more long trips and for months I didn't give this a thought. Until the day I found myself forced, under I don't know what circumstances, to notice that I had already begun to be able to think that soon I wouldn't take any more long trips. The idea of leaving my mother, of leaving myself without my mother for too long, that is for a week, the idea of finding myself detained at one of those several thousand kilometer distances that one can't cancel out, the idea of not being able to dash across the Allée Samuel Beckett, had finally got the best of the idea that one must not tempt the representations of anguish, which is an idea my mother has always strictly upheld, me forever in the grips of the worst case scenario, my mother on the other hand always siding with what's sane, bright and practical. You're the one who's sick, says my mother. I admit it. So I sided with the spirit of my mother against my personal penchant for gloom right up to the day I began suddenly to say that *soon – bientôt –* I would stop going away on long trips, which might be seen either as a concession to my anguish or as finding a way to stay at my mother's side. I spent a long time musing about the word *bientôt*, whose limpness contrasts with German's forceful *Bald*. Similarly I weighed: "long" and "a long time," interminably. I was trafficking in thousands of kilometers, the means of transport, all those factors that reduce, lengthen, objectively in appearance the images of traveling. What's more the inner schedule, the mental jet lags – all these things undergo daily shifts. I got just as mixed up in my calculations as the narrator of the useless automobile. If one day I were to give in, if I get the best of her – the she that my mother is inwardly allied with – I don't see myself saying to my mother: "I won't take any more long trips," I told myself. If I were to say that it would mean I didn't see, didn't hear the ghost of my mother's long voyage, toward which horror and madness drag me, stealing in behind this decision.

What's the word for when you keep yourself from speaking about something – when you stop yourself from talking about the thing that baffles words, tears – reticence? – I ask myself, no, reticence must have another name to hide behind, I tell myself, I don't know, I don't know, I could feel my thought stifled, bewildered, bogged down, no sooner poured out than filled to the brim again with bitter images, from the end of 2003 right up to January 2006. One fine morning I'm convinced I'm going mad. It's my darling balding old cat. I'd do anything in the world for her. I utterly adore this gaunt, aging, once-lovely creature, her pelt, but not her soul, worn with age. But while I'm chatting with the lady who runs the café about the wars and betrayals that the times have rendered global, the cat goes out. I dash after her. Across the wide street she goes to get hit, the way she'd cross a field, with a rapidity that proves the extreme purity of a desire. I dash after her. You would see us go by without slowing down, me not taking my eyes off her. I realize I've left all my worldly belongings in the café, my bag on the chair with my coat, my papers. But this would not bring our race to a halt. My old cat is the world to me. Where are you off to? I ask. I am crossing the city. How far would we have got if I hadn't caught up with her again at the corner of a street, captured by a boy, in a cage like a dog on a leash? Naturally I smash everything in sight. I'm going to kill you I tell the crook. If I had to I would. At which point I give the world back to my old cat. I could not do otherwise. Her happiness counted more than mine. Did she run off again? I'll never know. I was yanked from my dream by the sound of brakes screeching. The fateful noise. I didn't have time to see the end coming.

So I call my mother, and just as the phone rings I see that

it is the middle of the night for her. Already my mother, who during the day so often fails to hear, already my mother, with her hoarse old hen voice, hurrying toward me. – Mama! (What else to say, this is madness.) – Yes mydaughter!? her small high-perched voice. Do you want me to come? How did she guess? – Yes! says the dreamer who left everything in the café, the papers, sense of restraint, reason, discretion, incredulity, resignation. – I'll be right there, my mother signs off. When it comes to miracles reality is more powerful than dream.

– Next year. I said. I change. I can't do otherwise. I stop. I give death a sad wave of recognition. –You're rrright, whispers the shadow of a voice that exhausts itself climbing back up Ève's throat, I imagine the effort, the ascent of an old scarab, the steep cliff crumbling. Go for it, voice! The gymnastics it takes so as to be able to say – so early, for it is a long time yet till day, so late: "Stop running so we can still have a walk together while I am still able to walk" – just a little further

THE VITRINE

"There's no future" my mother thinks, she says this behind my back, she thinks I don't see her thinking this colorless, shapeless thing, that shakes out its rag full of terror in slow motion in a scene that has vanished without leaving an address, she thinks I don't see her scaring herself behind my back, furthermore the words of the sentence get ahead of her thoughts, they turn up, all of a sudden they pour in, they clog, this is what frightens her, this horrid, peremptory sentence, most unlike her, that turns up in a corner of her room at ten o'clock in the morning as she tries to wake, to get up, applying herself to the task of putting herself back together as once ninety years ago she would have trudged to school after a nightmare, she skirts the gluey verge of the road where once again she's missed the bus toward the day that has been here for hours already, still moving uncertainly, faceless and toothless, toward the little youthful old lady whom she is going to shower and comb and put on for the day, she's preparing to climb aboard this day dated June 15, 2007 she can

do it, June 15, she girds her loins with the waffle weave towel, everything needs to be done as usual, first empty the chamber pot, therefore first sit down and think, "there's no future" says the sentence, "what kind of stupid thing is that?" says my mother, she hasn't put her teeth in yet so the sentences hiss and mumble, but in her head this can be heard loud and clear, for the third time, the phrase rings out with the help of a stubborn little force, my mother ssslips into her ssslippers and brushshes off frttffrt the nasty spluttering sentence, she doesn't see it, from the glass cabinet where mama's little people pell-mell, the riddle-altar she alone has the keys to, indecipherable save by her immutable perennial self, and over which Omi's photo reigns.

"Here I shall insert a portrait of the glass cabinet: the Vitrine, *V*."

The idea that we have a vitrine in a "conventional" bourgeois interior has nothing at all to do with my mother's Vitrine.

For thirty years exactly – ever since my mother inherited the bedroom on the death of her mother, Omi, my German grandmother, whom she had moreover relinquished to me for mama herself never in my hearing called her anything other than "Omi," hence grandmother – each time I go past the V I look the other way. This is a sign that something in the Vitrine keeps me at arm's length. It doesn't want. Clearly it is secret. To see the face of the secret is not to see the secret, naturally, it is to see its mask. A mask is a face that hideshows, a mask mocks. A mask speaks volumes, that is, too much, not enough and nothing at all. A knot of beings huddle in the mask. It is like a dream trapped in a net of daylight and dried up. This bothers me. I don't know how many genies have nested in that wooden box that is neither a coffin nor a museum but like them has something of the domestic tomb.

I've been thinking for a while now that I should, for once,

avoid avoidance. A moment of introspection. Reciprocal. See the Vitrine, see myself seeing it, and see myself pale in its window, face up to it I mean offer myself the sacrifice, to the sacrifice, in sacrifice, "the time has come" I've been saying to myself lately. This means that a "toolate" might be in the offing.

For a while now, I've been looking at it askance, I think in zigzags, ricochets, indirectly, I come at it crabwise, I say "the time has come" so that I don't say something else, *the other thing*, in front of it I make a wall of curtains, I kick it out of my room, the thing that is other, the number of words I employ between the other thing and my window grows bigger each day it's not that I mean to annihilate it, no, I will never reach the nullity of nothingness, but keep it away, invent detours ricochets substitutes, this I do, and the energy I invest in the tricks I come up with to *trick myself* is not without its soothing effect. It's not much but it's better than nothing. True, my invention of flight may have a deleterious effect: today I suffer less, tomorrow maybe I'll suffer twice as much because I will regret not having done yesterday that which tomorrow become today, and today alas yesterday, I cannot and will never again for the rest of my days on earth be able to do. It's too late, I'll tell myself, I should have asked mama, but I couldn't not not ask. I should make a list. Two things stop me. (1) The idea that the idea of drawing up a list is caused by *the thing* I don't want to get its foot in the door. (2) Each time, at the end of a debate during which I turn this way and that to the point of exhaustion, at the sight of myself deciding to make a list, I'm so exhausted I forget what I wanted to ask mama. The Vitrine is one example. Nothing more obvious. Nothing more effaced. It holds me off. I hold it off. Nonetheless it must keep some precious objects in there behind its pane of glass, while a troubled discretion has hold of me, it's as if in her absence I had found her teeth in a glass.

Rather than putting it off the minute it comes to mind, I should insert an inventory of the Vitrine right here, without letting anything (convention, resistance) hold me back. The mere fact that I should so long have abstained from Vitrine makes the incitation all the stronger: I'll do it, here goes:

When you enter the room in which my mother is in her mother Omi's place it stands against the wall to the right. I am sitting to the right of the Vitrine in the Impossible Armchair which, incapable of accepting a human body without violence, serves as a clothes-horse. Therefore I don't see the Vitrine. I ask my mother for an inventory

I project my voice straight ahead, loud: Mama! She answers: My daughter! I say: *Stand here in front of the Vitrine* and tell me what's in it. I articulate. My mother stands, saddles her ass and comes to the glass-fronted cabinet. – I haven't put my ears on! says my mother. – We don't need them, I say. Speak I say. Pause. She's not hesitating. She's taking her inner mark. My mother always looks for: the method. Not *do* but *do well*. Find the exact place. At once. "During the war," she is thinking – standing in front of the Vitrine she is wearing Omi's little pink dressing gown, as in the days of my last war, find the right way to do it, I'm always doing three things at once, one thing makes me think of another, similarly in one life three lives all together at once, so then George said to me: Ève. Since he had to stop working because Jews weren't allowed, but me since I was nothing I could. He says: Ève. I stand up. I say: show me how. And George hands me a nice lean piece of horse meat. Here, the intra-muscular goes in the outer third of the buttock and not in the sciatic nerve. I have to give a lady a shot, says George. In I go good day madam, I could see she was scared but I'm not scared, I stick the needle in, the right place, she didn't feel a thing and out I came, after that I was at the house of a lady with post-partum dementia everything she says she has to say it in verse. Now let's have a go at the Vitrine. She can see that I am scared and she is not scared.

I say: mama. She executes. In her utter simplicity, which this moment must serve as an example of, my mother trusts, trusts her daughter implicitly. In these circumstances, which transport me with secret pride, I feel my mother's unselfconscious magnitude and love. She doesn't obey, she doesn't object, she doesn't tremble. I will come back to this later. Contents of the Vitrine as enumerated by my mother

She dictates, I write:

A salt-cellar

And this is a salt-cellar too

(We note right away from the pace and variations in the performance that the reciter *is discovering* the Vitrine. Right to the end she will express neither opinion nor emotion of any sort.)

(After and-this-is-a-salt-cellar-too, a pause – then: bang!)

Over here is a rooster from Tunisia

The photos I don't know (meaning: not from Tunisia)

Bric-à-brac: here's a pretty porcelain thing there's a key in it don't know where it comes from

Theres even a Hanukkah what's the point

We're never here in winter

No idea what's in this box

One more pretty thing I don't know where it comes from

China it looks like no Longwy France, someone broke it on me

Photo of Omi

A salt-cellar with something wrong with it

This is a little house from Amsterdam

Back in the back I wonder what that is

Unless it's *also* an oil lamp

From Tunisia? I say. From Morocco she says

A little crystal vase for a little flower

51

Here's a liqueur glass do you want it?

I look at mama's face, "and this too is a salt-cellar" I tell myself, her untroubled freedom to exist without explanations that gives these objects, cut off from whatever uses they had, a glow of mysterious consecration, these where's-that-froms that have come to the end of their aimless migrations under a pane of glass. What's left of the salt from my mother's grand worldwide travels. What's to become of these things these martyrs of who-knows-where, sorts of keys to no known doors?

"*There's no future*" my mother is thinking "I'd have thought the contrary, for me the future exists" what a funny thing to say, one is sipping one's coffee and all of a sudden a sentence turns up. The sentence might come from Omi maybe we're standing in for her, we sleep in her bed, we don't use the armchair she didn't use, maybe it's a letter from Omi to her daughter, now more advanced in age than Omi was. But why *in French* the sentence? My mother doesn't recognize Omi's style at all, it reminds me she thinks of that fake letter George dictated to Alice our house medium, a letter sent from beyond the tomb on the fourth floor to me on the second floor, right away I saw it wasn't his style, bombastic, no, he didn't write like that. Then that made me think of Jeanne, my cousin, each time I say something she says the opposite. Éri too, I say zig she says zag. Anyway There's no future is an interesting sentence I can't translate into German, this makes me think, she thinks, that is (1) this makes me think and (2) this makes me think by association, for that's how I really like to think now that I will soon be a hundred years old she thinks, I really like to think by association, I don't think verti-cally I think thoughts that touch each other attach spread out join up, it's the best way never to stop, never lose anything find things again, thinks my mother it's very interesting, I begin with one thought and it makes an underground bus

I can cross the whole world like this forever getting lost one never knows where one is but one thing leads to another, I notice there's the masculine and the feminine, with my son and my daughter, one always manages to blaze a trail back toward the light of day, what a long way round one goes, so now it must be time I got back to the surface of life, *ich bin ein alter Maulwurf* (I am an old mole), I always manage to find my way back out of the old stories, *man wird so alt wie ein Kuh doch lernt man immer zu*, I notice there are lots of animals in my thoughts, I still have a lot to learn about myself despite my advanced age I've never met myself, such a waste of time, it's others who interest me: *"There's no future!"* what's *that* all about? in any case *that* doesn't go away, that takes the wind out of my sails, look that tunnel is closed, it reminds me of the metro stop that doesn't exist – then my mother gets her gear, finishes herself, checks herself over, puts on the clunky, stabilizing shoes, puts her ears which are the ears of her ears on, pokes her long nose up into the half-light. *Mole*. It sniffs the eternal earth. And digs. If there's no future here we'll just keep moving. Her broad square hands nails worn away by the rubbing of time. How not weep? If I were sitting next to mama telling me do you need all these books, you need to earn your living, you could get married, that old suitor there with his tailcoat and top hat has a lot to recommend him you should give it some thought already I'd be fuming. But here I sit beside Grace herself, in the daylight I see how used up she is, how faded, worn down, if by night she finds again the laws of her youth, if she leads me and drags me along, upon waking the wrinkled cloth awaits her, nobody is allowed to spend their whole life at night. Ahead of me, the day is short, my mother rises at the end of the morning, at break-fast which takes the place of lunch two doors are open onto the table, the door of the moment, instant paradise, whose insignia is the Ricoré tin, which opens onto the door of Hell.

53

Between the two doors, the width of the table. Everything is delicious everything that is sweet turns to salt in my mouth. Everything is given-to-me-taken-away. I live by your grace, I say. Everything that is given-me-taken-away you give me.

Under the table my left leg clamped to her right leg. Just think: the one person in the world who will never betray me will betray me. Her nut-brown squirrel face. Chews, chewed. Summers I live on my mother shore, *au bord de ma mère*. I will betray me myself.

– Is everything all right, dear? My mother bends to the shore of my thoughts. – When you are here, I say. – I am right here. – Yesterday you said the opposite. Yesterday, sad, mama, little, bird, in the same place, said: "I've done my time." *Ich bin alt und klapperich.* – *Was heißt klapperich?* – I search. She searches. *Klapperich.* It's like a little rag doll. Then I forgot. She bursts out laughing.

I sit on Lethe's quay the daughter of Discord and the mother of Grace, I discord myself, thinking I hear mama's skeleton crack in my skeleton arms.

This book is called Lethe *here.*

To think that everything that I think I'm experiencing approaching caressing keeping losing once summer is over will be forgotten, I'll remember it in other words. With words that astonish, attempt to nail time's canvas to the wall. Aletheia sleeps on my right, keeping watch, the way cats sleep, saying: while I sleep every hair is wide awake

My mother ruminates. I look at my mother. She thinks straight ahead to the tree at the window. Below the thought thought right in front of her on the table, something is thinking deeper down, in the dark, it is digging away I see evidence of the digging, it is grinding its jaws, it moles and moles, night and night, everything is always night. Chews on a thought hidden in her bread, under it, now it's in the foliage, suddenly

54

my mother sees the worm in the leaf. – *Jeden Tag hab ich ein Dorn im Auge*. – Which needle is in the eye of today? – It's the branch. That branch is dead. It's not pretty. It's part of nature. Thinks the thought. – Do you see the future in the tree? She bursts out laughing. See the future? Having it in her eye makes her split her sides laughing. She wipes her eyes. It makes me cry laughing. She weeps laughter. I weep a little. I make a note. I'll forget this branch, the dead branch will die, I don't know when the future will be, the future of the dead branch that makes my mother laugh to tears because for a moment she sees herself clambering up into the tree and removing this thorn from her eye, for a moment she sees herself dead, swaying in the wind, I make haste to collect the trace in a notebook that my mother bought me at the supermarket and thus will have bought for me, but maybe this notebook hasn't, will not have, any future anterior at least no future future anterior. The future anterior's behind us. My mother chuckles I have a quick cry. I won't reread it, it won't be read in my lifetime, another thorn in the eye of the soul, and all this is part of nature. My mother bursts out laughing. I have never *acted upon* my future. It has always been a surprise to me . . . says my mother. And vanishes. Where has she gone? I think passionately of the mole, where is she thinking, what, maybe in the tunnel underneath the table, maybe she's left me, she disappears without warning and I won't even know about it? The mole idea persists. Her devastation is my pain and my enchantment, I tell myself, it is like death and the idea of death, a thing, an idea, a creature of *some sort*. Under along what I fear and want not to run away from. I have lived so long underalong my father mole, my very own Morpheus, my dear father a specialist in the art of reassuming appearance, gait, features, in his eyes a chaste smile, each time he dons the pearl grey suit or the white doctor coat, and does a perfect imitation of himself, no trickery, when he shows up it's a big occasion, but we are always torn for we are not unaware that he is still dead and only on a short-term loan to love. All the same, pain doubles the joy of this visit and gives him a super-natural quality, everything is twice over, twice the joy twice the sorrow, twice the love. We are dead and living nonetheless. I'm used to it. I know the signs. Who'd have thought a very different mole would come along later, a species as different from the Mediterranean mole as the star-nosed mole, so that initially and for several years I will not recognize it, I will not understand its goings on, fooled by the rapidity of my mother's outings (gotoJeanne's and back) and by the rosy flush of her cheeks as she is chatting to me about her outing, and me never for a minute getting wind of the secret under my very nose, I record her comings and goings without noticing in my mother's incessant errands a less grandiose, more discreet version of a crossing of the fatal strait.

"... that reminds me," says my mother mole. She's tougher than us. What a vast domain she has underneath the earth! She's not afraid of the dark. What can make them go so far? She doesn't even keep her eye peeled for the exit that's the best part, mole my mother. Whereas we, when we tunnel we look for the way out. God knows what's under ground in the way of creatures I don't know. I know it makes holes but. Such excursions are unimaginable. Man is really modest, he makes one last little hole and that's it. But the mole has a boundless domain that no one envies. – I think he overdoes things, says my mother. Ambition has its limits. Indefatigable is all very well. But this is absurd says my mother. – You don't agree with God? – I keep my feet on the ground, not yet underground says my mother. Could we *go-to-Jeanne's?* asks my mother. – We'll have to take the metro, says my mother. I myself prefer the above-ground bus. As far as my mother is concerned there's a connection between go-to-Jeanne's and go-underground. Little by little without noticing we sink into the thin, broken crust of this conversation. Our phrases quiver, my mother lifts her nose, crumbs stick to her upper lip. – Lick, I say. – Go-to-Jeanne's on the metro is faster. – Lick, I say. She doesn't hear me. She is digging herself a tunnel deep underground, she shovels, scoops, sifts, scrapes, blows, in her mine she must be getting close to the Rothschild Foundation. Where cousin Jeanne drifts like the wrack thick on Lethe's quay. What a shame if I can't tunnel into her mine I tell myself. Gently I destrange her. "Mama!" Here we are nose to nose tunnel and mine. Her mine's eyes fly open. On my face she *sees* her deafness: my lips move to no avail. A shudder of laughter. "Oh! what fun! You are off with words and speech, sending them to the moon, and where I am I can't hear a sound!" She lifts her little subterranean turtle head and sends a salvo of laughter heavenward. We laugh.

– Mama! I say. – I'm-drinking-my-coffee! says my mother. That means: I'm just dandy. She says I'mdrinkingmycoffee with a triumphantly tender smile, it's a love letter. I receive it. One day I'll write the book of utterances signed mama, I tell myself, complete with translation, an inventory of their secret usages, and above all indications as to the intonations, all this subtle and singular linguistics that makes my mother's speech a very powerful and original composition underneath its modest dress. This will be difficult, somewhere between onomatopoeia and epic, maybe we'll call it *happ*, Happ as in Hoo! As in Ève! showing the *surprise* the pounce of the happnimal upon life, or the sudden dive through the paws of death. Happ! there she goes! That sudden brutal movement of a *pounce*, that one also finds in the Germanic languages. – *Happ!* what do you think of *happ?* I say. Mama laps up her coffee. –Happ? It's half of *happy*. Only dogs hapse like that. Me, I lapse! She chuckles into her coffee.

– Whereas Jeanne, says my mother, never happy, forever complaining and her cheerful sister, always moaning and groaning, she's outlived them all. Whereas Jeanne is the last of the family. She didn't have any children. Jeanne remains. Ève remains. Last of the Kleins. Decline of the Kleins.

"I'm drinking my coffee" next I'd make sure the different melodies were audible how one may be close to a sudden swelling of the *Fifth Symphony* and how "I've drunk my coffee" might be compared to the Wagnerian leitmotif of a Evalkyrie. And always something Happ! lively, brutal, with the ring of sporty female androgyny.

Go-to-Jeanne's for my mother signifies traveling a short distance under the ground while remaining above the ground or vice versa remaining above ground while for an hour or so testing the conditions of a halt midway between the surface and the start of the underground. The go-to-Jeanne theme sounds at first like the visit of one old cousin, my mother, to another old cousin, Jeanne, more or less the same thing in a different setting. For Jeanne, installed at last in the retirement home at the Rothschild Foundation, is the halfway house. In truth go-to-Jeanne's is much more complicated than it appears. The thoughts that precede and traverse the visit ramify into a network beyond the reach of any attempt to inventory or calculate them. Go-to-Jeanne is the name of a station in one of my mother's typical dreams. It's not that far, but something always makes it *to the ends of the earth: au diable Vauvert*. The *Diable Vauvert* is also the name of a station sacred to my mother's unavowable cult of the French language. When I was working in the lawyer's office. That's the diable Vauvert. To start with I imagine the Devil is a worm, *un vers*, it's a worm we want. Going to the diable Vauvert consists in a warped kind of feat in which one rejoices in managing to go somewhere one hasn't the slightest desire to go.

All my life, thinks my mother, I've got the best of the diable Vauvert. Getting the best of the devil in my mother's speech means: having brutally met up with death and sent it packing. When the devil comes your way, don't run away, don't confront him head-on either, I have always preferred to avoid him, says my mother, maybe this is a flaw, maybe not. I don't look for trouble. I'd rather slip between his teeth and be done with it. *Once* with pneumonia last year I levitated behind the bed and whoo! he didn't get me. I can't tell you where the diable Vauvert comes from. It's awfully far and you can be sure not many people go there. Vauvert is far that's all. In the old days they thought the devil was a fellow with claws for feet. I've never been convinced by the supernatural. Far, we don't know where it is. I was living under the *Toit Familial, The Family Roof.* I worked on the rue Vaugirard. That's where I came across this Vauvert. Vau to rhyme with toe. At Mr Müller's, the lawyer, who sends me off with a letter to the diable Vauvert. I don't know if you can find yourself in all that. Not to worry I find myself everywhere. When I came back to the Toit Familial, I was shaking my mop out, says my mother. I stop her. – What's the Toit Familial? – It's a Rothschild Foundation residence for girls living on their own in Paris. There was a big table. Each girl had a box. It was full of tonics. These girls with the tonics had a goal. They wanted to become civil servants. In Germany Jews don't become civil servants. I was the adventurous one.

Hence everything has always already begun with the place they call the Rothschild Foundation. Places don't talk. One says *Le Toit Familial* "a residence for girls from good families" and the fiction has begun. The Entry into the World. *Ève and Éri Take Paris. Studies of Manners*, Studies of Tomb. – We need to walk fast, says Ève, otherwise we'll never get any-where. – Ève tells me, look, there's the Tower, we go straight ahead, says Éri. Afterward we walked straight ahead down the street and next thing we were at the Bazaar de l'Hôtel de Ville, BHV. All I bought was a pair of pajamas I didn't like says Éri. – That took the better part of two afternoons. First

we went. Then we took them back, says Ève. – Just three
times to the movies and three times to museums, says Éri. –
Éri's never satisfied, says Ève. Tomorrow we go Chez Jeanne.
Exit the World through the same door. My mother doesn't
say: the Rothschild Foundation. She says: gotoJeanne's.
She expresses her desire to gotoJeanne's discreetly, almost
absent-mindedly, for months I might think it's a false idea, a
whim, the sort of wish that can vanish overnight. Maybe she
doesn't even know herself whether she wants to gotoJeanne's.
She puts it off. It would of course be easier to go on the spur
of the moment, on a day she happens to be in the neighborhood. But since it's to the end of the earth – *au Diable* – a
decision is required.

Ève, Éri, they don't know. They don't know where they're
off to when they get up in the morning and saddle their ass
to *GotoJeanne's*. As far as my mother is concerned, since this
leitmotif has gone from whim to obsession these past few
years, I would guess *GotoJeanne's* means keeping her feet on
the ground while going to see what it's like in the underground for a bit. Each time my mother, and even more her
sister, expresses the wish to gotoJeanne's it is in order to
exercise this faculty of imagination she denies having that
lets us see where we stand as regards death's propositions
without our being conscious enough not to jump back. My
mother feels the urge to return to the original Toit Familial
just as I can't not go back to Montaigne's Towers in order
to size myself up. Still, these two compulsions face opposite
ways. My mother must go to the Toit at each intimation of
mortality. A way of bidding farewell founded on the hypothesis that one of the two cousins could be extinguished in the
course of the year, the chances of this being objectively equal
on both sides. Whereas I go to Montaigne to resign, as is
done in my religion, the act of immortality. In the old days
the urge to return to the original Toit was brought on by a

60

well-tempered politeness of the heart, my mother still having eight earthly cousins among whom to pick and choose. Then there are six, and all of a sudden two. Each cousin with sister becomes a sister without her sister. I try to picture the scene of the meeting between the Last of the Kleins but no picture comes to mind. I see them waiting for one another on the Quai de la Gare, peering around, they don't find one another

– Last time we went-to-Jeanne's with Éri, says my mother. That was a year ago. It's a long trip. We took the metro at Denfert. Éri didn't want to go. The day I can't get around on my own any more I'll go there, it's magnificent. The garden, I can't get over it.

This story is a mother-lode, I was telling myself, hiding in the pitch black of my tunnel I tried to collect the involuntary thoughts as involuntarily as possible. This was last year, I let myself be led through the swerves of the conversation now my mother taking the lead now her sister.

– There was *nobody but Jeanne around* says Éri.

– The ladies get up late says Ève.

– In the Manchester home we are up and about after breakfast. Éri barks at death. Upright on the banks of Lethe.

– Let me tell you something: those people were in another room we didn't see. My mother on the other bank

– If there is a room, *das Kann mal wohl sehen*. The room we didn't see, in vain Éri repeats her complaint

– We didn't ask where it was

– I saw two who were all alone in a wheelchair. The man was spinning the wheels, feet dragging on the ground – *Oh horrible! Oh horrible! Most horrible!*

– A huge orchard, lots of trees

– Those primitive chairs! *What falling off!*

– Then we went out for Chinese food

– Oh there was much too much to eat!

– We were the last customers

61

– Since it was twenty-two euros says my mother, I had only a fifty-euro bill, out of fifty what's my change?

– A ten-euro bill and underneath it a five-euro bill.

– Oh I'm sorry I got it wrong says she says my mother. In my opinion you don't get it wrong says my mother. Wrong *me* maybe, but not *yourself.*

– Being as we're nearly a hundred years old it was worth a try, says Éri.

– And what do you think about that my daughter? You're the one who always says we shouldn't always be keeping accounts. There's a limit all the same.

– She counted our age.

– Why do you think she did that? Someone who spends her whole day at a cash register? To me that's unacceptable.

No doubt, when I piece this story together later, I will be able, from my fairly detailed notes and memories, lit up, I tell myself, by me, with the funereal gleam of the Foundation where I note I have never been, and which consequently has the virtual visual substance of those sorts of extraordinarily ominous places that I see myself constructing in my dreams, like those awful, opulent hotels, their soft staircases carpeted in purple, in which they put me up, to do me honor they say, in rooms so lofty so remote that I never find them unless I tell myself with the anguish of Alcyone that I must without further delay telephone you my love and beg you to come and stay with me, in this place whose eeriness makes me fear the worst, but which never at any moment of my ascension offers me a chance of finding a phone, this is not a hotel I moan it's a trap set by the spirit of hospitality, whose great red gullet ingests whatever guests it attracts. Right after having overcome the Devil of Pneumonia, my mother gets up. We meet her again on the Champs-Élysées with Éri then right afterwards despite Éri's reticence on the Champs-Élysées once again but under the name of Foundation. But since I am the only one who knows this odysseyesque mythology, I'll keep to myself the *Unheimlichkeit* feeling that casts its pall over me: they are off all unawares to the kingdom of the dead just as I see myself put up in the five-star plush Hotel Rome the very day I have an appointment at six o'clock back home with my friend who is still living about which I can only rejoice while grievously deploring my being absurdly retained in this Grand Hotel Rome by an incongruous and totally inexplicable whim of hospitality. When I finally understand that Rome is not in Rome and when I remember that mor is, it's too late, the hour for our meeting has passed. Whereas my two elderly characters will never know one place hides another

I will be able, when I understand, I tell myself, what prophetic vibrations a hair-raising story might contain, just as the porcupine crown on Hamlet's head signals a presentiment, whose forlorn colors may be legible later, the previous year having come to an abrupt halt with the hasty ablation of Éri, swept off the stage of time with a briskness only a few works of fiction manage to render with the sort of dryness and brevity that makes one tremble – those of Balzac or Ovid for example where the slow pace of the storytelling gives way from one line to the next to a torrent – and as I am to note in retrospect a great number of allusions to "the end" in all the adventures of Éri and Ève last year – I will be able to insert a few lines discreetly sprinkled with Ovidian lamentation, I will say something like: "With these words, as if she had a presentiment of what the future held, Éri shivers and finally utters: it's all up for me"

Better to make the connection with my mother when the two characters interpreted by my mother and my aunt immediately afterwards act what I call "The Argument," a sequence I have written to emphasize the way two people can live their lives on two stages at once, the one actual, spontaneous, the first draft, the other, simultaneous and consubstantial, "improvised" by the same beings as actors, that is persons made of two fabrics, instantaneously reflected, the reflection and the action the ricochet from the one to the other taking place at the very same second, as is also somewhat the case for a writer who muses about himself, reflects himself back to himself at the very same time when he isn't reflecting, as if his nature or naturalness by definition being tremulous, he were forever echoing in his very phraseology a third party self. Thus on condition of or as a result of being for decades observed by me, my mother and my aunt had made of themselves sorts of delectable actresses whom they would have decried and disavowed had they noticed them, who weren't exactly them but really and truly them with only a hint of exaggeration, like a strange intoxication that came over them and made their cheeks flush and their eyes sparkle. Or maybe they barge into my study, set me up as judge in wig and robe, and although they don't realize that we are in the little Heilbronn courthouse, they act like born plaintiffs. And these actresses they were unaware of being – it was they who prompted them to be more dramatic. I've filed these pages in the royal blue cardboard box, the obvious choice for the purpose (*Éri and Ève Acts Symptomatic and Accidental*) into which I cram without order or chronology, as into a child's toy box, all the trinkets I glean. Therefore whenever I "consult" this file, it's a box of tricks. I open. I don't find. No problem. I rummage, there's enough here to fill three volumes, I don't find, I don't, and I see this is going to cost me a whole morning of despair and nervous exhaustion, for right away I recognize the urge that makes the object that escapes me the absolute ruler of my life and fate. This means – I'll tell myself when I emerge hours later all but drowned in my own shortcomings – I'm at the mercy of my marionettes, they govern my fate and, even if I'm sure I've locked them up in the handsome royal chest, they are elsewhere and bent on proving – thrown off scent – if I'd wished – or maybe – in the yellow notebook – what a mess – waste my time on junk – this desperate search, I could die of if I had my mother's arrhythmia – and maybe somebody in my mother is not averse to making me feel the throes – has at least for secondary effect that of reminding me of the mystery of the things we call precious and which are precious in proportion to the price we are willing to pay to make use of them, every inch of my soul and all the desires I have invested in my mother and accessorily in Éri and metonymically in the pots and pans and the bric-à-brac of the one or the other, different, which on the one hand deserve to be trashed and on the other hand make it worth my while to go and rummage in the bin just in case I thought I by mischance threw out one of mama's rubber gloves or one of the edicts jaundiced with age used to post her wishes in all the common rooms of the house, resulting in this or that scrap of paper (whose format speaks worlds of my mother-who-wastes-nothing's spirit of thrift) having acquired, at least within the city limits of my heart, for having brightened for over thirty years the bathroom with the untiring tone of her command, thus: *no sand in the bathtub*, the importance and value of a Hantaï canvas upon which the great artist has set down, in among the folds, the bunchings, the accidents that carry the creative act beyond itself, an unanalyzable condensation of traces and thoughts stubbornly sucked from the philosophical honeys, that forms the invisible but vital deposit composed of time, the saliva of books and dreams, grunts of anger, battles ever re-begun against SAND (*sable*), which is the name of the demon of negligence, of homogeneity, of psychic dust, of the agglomeration of distinct elements that forms the nobility of art, but which even as it is banished, swept out, and because requiring strength, attention, labor, is truly part of the whole from which it is expelled, and mingles its reign *Çableux*, sabulous, sandy, its

65

unqualifiable *Ça*, its Itness, with life itself, in whose heart it causes these events of a mind-boggling singleness

when I'll have looked in vain in the blue file, to the point of reaching the pale quay of renunciation, after having first wreaked havoc on my desk, and maybe on the occasion of this havoc those pages will slide out of a yellow folder without a name, just as my cats have a way of turning up when, having been called and sought for a long time, a painful seeking to which their response an inexorable non-response they don't come out of hiding places whose secret will never be told. All of a sudden: there they are.

ARGUMENTS

– Let's argue, says Ève. – All right, says Éri. Arguments are the spice of their life. The argument word is good for an argument too.

– But the coffee cup, says my mother, there was a lot of porcelain, never was I served such a big cup with nothing in it. The place packed with people. Coffee with milk and a croissant. No coffee. Croissant. Éri couldn't eat: there wasn't any butter. No butter. Éri says: *I* need a big meal and *she* orders a croissant. You see how she is says Éri, you see how she is says Ève. I don my judge's wig, I listen, *She* sent it back, who, I say, what, *She* ordered it, that dish, *She* sent it back, *You* didn't want it. But what business is it of yours, what I eat or don't eat. You. You see how we fight. *She* had the plate in her hand, *She* sent it back. I didn't feel like eating a big plate of food. It had two slices of roast beef. I say you'll eat the second slice. Maybe, but I can't eat roast beef. So you see. I saw *three* frying pans I wanted to buy I didn't buy. Everything on sale. *So.* She wanted the frying pans she didn't buy. I wanted to buy. Three pans and I can throw out the old ones. I didn't want to carry them. I would have carried them, we were right at the bus stop. *Three* frying pans! Just what we needed. Three caskets says the judge. *Pans*, say the characters. Three frying pans, fifty euros. Not written anywhere. How much they were marked down from. *So*. You don't know whether it's one euro cheaper than before. If it's on sale it's written before so much now this. So you see. We didn't go to check. Home we go without any frying pans. We could have come home with pans and we come home without. It's stupid. This isn't a very exciting conversation. A beautiful art show across the street. We didn't go. Lots of people waiting in line. That's a good sign. We went to the wrong show. Now those picture frames: what made you bring those frames here? – Who on earth would come to my house and leave such stuff? – They are really horrible. Some people like Such Stuff. If you don't like them give them to the cleaning lady. All the same I have to ask Jim. Americans like antiquey things. I have a water-pick at my place too. Throw it out. You've been talking about it for a year. You see. My son told me to use it. And I've still got all my teeth, says the dentist's mother. – My dentist said not to use it. So who to believe? – I don't want to believe your dentist. There are no hygienists in France. In England every three months I get my teeth cleaned. – In any case there was a dentist in your neck of the woods who was very dear twenty-five pounds ten years ago I still had ten teeth. You ought to see what she was earning that girl, remember? – I don't remember. – Well, I remember. It's the dentist who was cashing in. – Not at all the girl gets the money. – Now you remember. – *Chez nous* it's the dentist. – *Chez nous* it has nothing to do with the dentist. You see, *She* says *cheznous*. The minute there's a dentist involved it's *cheznous*. – Anything else? I say. With Éri you can always find something says my mother. – *Blödsinn*. – Now you have to pay us my mother says. That's enough blather. You think it's free? Where do these chocolates come from? – Someone gave them to me, I say. – Are they any good? Give them to Éri. – I don't want any chocolates. – See? *She* doesn't want any chocolates.

– Now we're leaving, says my mother. We're going into the book. All of us are on the point of departure. The old woman's old folks. I am going to go to your bookstore and tell the dealer: do you know who I am? I am Madame Cixous, the milk cow.

On the quay of the book, mama will say *she* would never have said "blather," *déblatérér*. Maybe Éri would have said it, with her uncertain French. *Blathering*'s what camels do, she says. The cow, on the other hand, makes her cry laughing.

TWO SLICES OF LIFE

The winds are the violent lords of Theory, says my friend. During the entire time of Theory, they blow, they blow imagination-roiling storms, trees bow to the earth, the roofs over family homes are blown away like the pages of notebooks, countries come out of this scalded by heat waves and are plunged into ironic yellow floodwaters teeming with the cadavers of calves and goats, sometimes they throw themselves down for one afternoon on the ravishing slopes of a meadow they doze off, they groom themselves like lions purring over their victims, giving mortals time to catch their breath and undergo fresh tortures. There in few words you have the ferocious laws of Theory. Theory is this sort of Weather. Horrible all the time with a clearing or two now and then so you can recharge your anxieties. During the Time of Mighty Winds a hundred times one thinks one is going to die one perishes over and over again, one thinks about *that* and nothing else, about her, about him, about the hour, all one thinks about is about not thinking about that, one kills oneself to death. She's going to go away and leave me, I tell myself, she is leaving me, I'll see her I say I hug her a hundred times, I see myself, again, the dreadful night I then spend, and not the first, it's the tenth, and the worst, yet I want to hold onto her. And the morning! No morning. May morning be incapable of getting up, of following in the footsteps of the sun! The Winds sit on the sides of the world. Then the word morning grows heavier and heavier, thickens, blares. Gong, knell, wings fled, no soaring through the branches of the pine, its thousand wings of free birds, its retinue of squirrel songs, its taste of honey and blackberries spread between the slices of pine, its burst of laughter ringing out again, I've too much past in my eyes, oh old walks that promise me: we won't be back, oh my friends, how they fall around me and with them carry off shards of the universe, an innumerable fabulous impoverishment, I could list them, famous cities, taken, yanked away, the world's most beautiful conversations. I feel sorry for myself, I feel sorry for myself all by myself, with whom else, mama is sleeping, when she wakes I can snuggle up to her, twist my heartstrings, every-one has been taken away from me, I will say, I am destitute, I've been raided, friends have given up en route, lands don't traipse after me any more, I am losing words, names, my voice poured out, I am hounded from paradise, the houses in which I was alive one after another have been boarded up, I live in fear of my deaths, no longer am I in the Canadas, the New York taxis disembark me, I could make an enormous list of my disinheritances what is Montaigne's word for recalling-to-memory? I no longer remember the names that call back, Time embalms me alive, tome after tome, my head's library erases itself, I've lost the balm of weather, Winds attack me, Oh I clutch my little old German tree, at least I try, she too? You are leaving me? I enter for ever into the tears, then

That's when I'll hear a loud scuffling noise, difficult

to imitate, something like old valets shuffling into the Guermantes courtyard, an insistent shuffling noise accompanied by the jolt of small-caliber, metallic wheels on the same surface. I translate: it's my mother's slippers, true animals creeping rather nimbly ahead on their blue felt bellies, advancing to the clicking of the wheels of a table she shoves ahead of her to keep herself upright, the harness of late morning. And my mother is. Oh mama, chipped Virgin, dawn-come-lately, this time it's past noon what sadjoy joysad I shall weep. I write these lines, much abridged, almost not saved, notebook spread at last on the blue-and-white-striped-oilcloth-mantle-of-the-hundred-year-old-Virgin-covered table, to the right of mama, who chomps. It's a slice of bread-and-butter almost the size of her face slathered with dark red jam. She adjusts the bread-and-butter between her dentures. Closes. Bites down. Looks at the world. Holds it. Sees the world. "Gorgeous, that red sea over there." A wide-angle view of the world in four pots of red geraniums. And it is gorgeous, I see it too. The red sea. It is gorgeous. Why? I say. The contrast with the darker greenery. This is how I crossed the red sea. Meanwhile the bread-and-butter. She shoves the slice of bread between her frail jaws and pulls. Pulls. Twists. A mouthful comes off. Chews. Smiles with her eyes. Beside her, I write. Slice of paper. She says nothing. I adjust. I pull. The broad page. – I have come back, says my mother. I had a stupid dream. I went to Spain. Right away I spent the money, not a penny left. This is a problem for in Spain you need money to come back. In Spain I had a clinic they took it away from me. Every now and then they take my clinic, it's never in Algiers, it is always somewhere else. One dreams the impossible things. Having nothing left to do, I woke up. – A miracle, I say. – Me I am like a shooting star that falls, and I get up again, who knows why. And all that without the fortifiers. I'm going.

71

She remains as enigmatic as ever to me. She is beyond. I don't know who she is. I don't know who knows who knows who she is. She is going on a hundred years. She wags her finger at me. Enough of your *Stimmung*. Doom and gloom. *Gloom* enchants her. Pirouette. – Don't worry about me. As long as I'm here I'm here. And when I'm not-here, I'll be not-here. *La vie tient à un fil*, as they say. *Je tiens à une fille*. Life hangs by a thread. I cling to my daughter. She laughs. So early in the day and already rhyming. What I wonder is: who will take my place in your life? I look around you, your friends. The thought of the place of the irreplaceable kills me. My mother looks around me. – Do you see anyone? I ask. And the tears pour out. – You aren't going weep ahead of time, oh come on! My mother doesn't weep in advance. But the whole place of living wisely is occupied by my mother. I thread a laugh into the tears. Weep afterward, not that either. I remember that, the not weeping ahead of time, in this strong impulse of love for the present absolute that is proof of her absolutely unique genius, my mother does not weep, for one only weeps by making overtures, which she of course rejects, to misfortune. I shall admire the way she can say without being boastful or redundant: as long as I am here I am here. Only she I tell myself inhabits a sparkling Iamhere, the needle in a haystack of time where shadows do not form.

– You're leaking says my mother. What's that seeping from your pen?

– The double waters of Lethe. Depending on which bank you drink from, they have different charms. I would like to ask her "the impossible," but with her that won't work. So I ask for *the maximum*. Who knows the *real* powers of our wishes that don't believe, that despair, but which all the same hope beyond hope for the improbable.

– Ten years! I say. Ten more years! For me!

Ten years I tell myself, I am aghast, I am dazzled by the

sentence, by the hope, the horror, the folly, it's a trifle, it's too much, I can see my death, ten years a few books two wars, a childhood, telling myself that's a whole *decade!* and the word burst in my mind, what did I say, I said to myself, I saw myself judge condemned torturer, this is what it's come to, what's more this is the least of it, I was about to say five years, I don't deny, the calculations outstrip me or maybe it's my heart ah! had I said five years tomorrow I was dead, I was assassinating or maybe it's the contrary, I take myself off to death and without having yet been called, *I* am the ultimatum, I am utterly miserable, a bank, a savings and loan, I shoot, I see the bullets, my mother falls or I do, so in ten years, a hundred and seven years old it's tomorrow, it's crazy, in October 2017 I dodder as if I wanted to outlive myself, fear makes a gambler of me, I encrime myself and I disaccord myself, I turn a comedy into a tragedy, and on top of all that to think that ten years make ten years! that they could be counted measured weighed sliced eaten with reason, and in short, endure, no, that's tantamount to believing nothing at all, thinking nothing it's like covering the pit of misery with a little word, a syllable, how despicable, also I am sorry mama has such a frightful daughter, I worry she whom I adore with my furious worrying, insatiable is what I am, and with what unfailing obstinacy I wean her of that which would make life easier for her, I refuse her peace of mind, each time she wants to get ready for her Voyage I am nowhere to be found, the documents she says, I have to show you, when you come, she says, tomorrow, I say, *the blue notebook*, says she, tomorrow I say, here she is on page 507 and I'm still reading the second chapter.

– Ten years, says my mother, is a great deal. I'm thinking: shall I give myself a little treat? Shall I eat this half-slice? She smiles me this half-slice. Must eat well she thinks, therefore must plan well eating and living, eating living, think eating, think living, I think everybody falls one never knows why

73

why not, everything holds by a thread, ten years, I'm going to treat myself but the thread is a very frail spider web. *Tenu.* Tenacious. What's the word? – *Ténu.* Tenuous? – Tenuous? All right: tenuous. Tenuous: she sucks on it. Tenuous. That's a good word, I like it. I don't know what It is holding on to since it takes so little for It to disappear. I hang on to life, therefore I am tenuous. Tenuous. The Tenuous is tenacious. And there you go.

I watch her eat think hold smile suck, work with her tongue. Live. I agree, she says. I don't know whether she is accepting the unacceptable. Or whether she's taking *the bet.* She's done. And to conclude, she darts a triumphant glance at the plate of English porcelain. Well! I showed them. Both *slices.* That's a lot. Down they went, just like that! The word slice lies on the plate. They say a slice of life, says my mother. Creation and duration, there's the mystery of life. Maybe if I didn't have a daughter which I have I would be less tenacious. Let me develop this thread. Those who die young, my mother reasons, have a flaw in their reasoning. Many flaws. Here's how. (1st case) Your father had he gone on being a chiropodist would be still alive. He didn't want to limit himself to feet? Do you have to climb the Himalayas on a bicycle when you are a doctor and frail? (2nd case) My father if he hadn't enlisted as a soldier would not have had his leg torn off, an iron cross in place of a life. He thought the Goodlord would protect him! No, no, don't count on the Goodlord. Think! (3rd case) David, Marga's grandson, such a nice boy always lending a hand, a doctor who dies too young through faulty reasoning. To think I thought of him not long ago, I had a cousin for him the only one who has a very kind heart, had he not gone off looking for adventure in Africa, do you have to prove What to Whom? What do they have in common? I am developing the thread of the knife, says my mother, none of them, no, they didn't meet, but (who's to say the contrary) they had to find death, they didn't stop living, no, before their time came they had to find it, that's what I object to. Does that strike you as natural? Off they go to put themselves to death, and for that, all the way to Asia, all the way to Russia, all the way to Zambia, doing whatever caught their fancy, I mean, reasons my mother, because all that is connected to feet, to deport oneself like that, with a displaced desire for the ground they haven't got their feet on they go to ridiculous lengths, in my opinion, look at animals, they live in groups, whereas this kind of men overly helpful men that tempt the devil again and again without so much as a second thought, it's unbelievable, we really don't live in the same world, from which they need to exclude themselves, and we're the ones who foot the bill, they have no idea the price of life. I call that taking the high road to suicide, do you get that, *I* don't get it. Konsider the Kourage it takes! I think the Kourage is fake. Those who make a faux pas on purpose, they never Konsider who pays for the Himalayas. I knew a rabbi, a refugee, who gave up an important project, because he made a misstep on his own threshold. He showed he was superior to the rest of us incredulous people, a better psychologist than your father. He saw immediately that this misstep proved the existence of a doubt, he was about to leave for Palestine, where he couldn't have earned a living, they don't need rabbis over there, he didn't have faith in himself, which would have destroyed the force of his intention when the time came to execute his project. Unfortunately he got tuberculosis and that was that. In conclusion I'll hang on *as long as I can.* But when it comes to the *invisible things* there's not a lot you can do.

More and more I am afraid more and more I love her, I make haste I store up all time's love or all the times of love, as if I were filling the Ark to come. But the Ark has a huge hole in its hull. But I pile up. But it's a waste of time, nothingness will swallow us up. But frantically I store up, and for nothing. I can't stop myself.

– Stop this feathering, says my mother. *Feathering* lives, wriggles, makes me laugh. Later on I'll wonder what the word was, I'll see the scene, the table, the oilcloth, my mother's latest coinage, I'll have forgotten it.

The ark has a crack, where the worms that chew our lives during our lifetimes come in. I caulk it.

I live on the edge of the abyss with my mother. A life that fear ravines, revives, stokes. I am in the first person singular, my mother too on her side.

An infinitesimal abyss inhabits the we that trembles between us. It is a patch of skin scraped off that suppurates on her hand and keeps her awake while I sleep on unaware of the pus. The injury toys with me. There is a lag before the scraped-off skin affects me, though I was but a step from the wound. With paper I try to caulk the cracks.

I don't deny the abyss, I attempt to imitate it, feebly, the only kind of medicine that might limit its populous empire. I read around these edges. The *Phaedo* makes me a little parapet. As if I were getting close to the original by acquainting myself with the copies.

HEMLOCK

– Do you know the death of Socrates? *La mort de Socrate?*
I ask. –Socrates' mother? *La mère de Socrate?* shouts Deafness
back. Know his mother? Of course not, my mother says. Here
we are, sitting on the balcony, my mother in white trousers,
me in paper, Cousin Deafness watches over us, Éri might
be here too, represented by the third rattan chair on which
last summer she left her paradoxical silhouette, an elegance
of her own confection to which her hump, which over any
other humpback might have cast a shadow, always gave an
added touch of chic, a beauty spot, as strangely effective as a
rosebud in a décolleté. I still see the wig, Éri's other beauty
spot. I see the chair and right away I see my aunt, ravishing,
with the charm of the pretty woman my aunt always was, to
the manner born, my mother would say, set off by those two
advantages, the hump and the wig, that she received with
grace like two extra gifts mother nature had granted her, I
see the chair and I see the yellow silk banner draped over the
hump. Éri: delectable at over ninety as under thirty Éri's were

the mysterious secrets of eternal youth, whereas my mother has the inner charms, I still see my aunt garnering glances, my mother looking on. My mother too sees the chair, and therefore Éri. And what are we thinking about do we think she and I? About death, that is about our dead, we feel them hovering under the diaphanous muslin curtains behind the armchairs, beneath the branches of wisteria, embalmer of our nostalgic musings ever since the first wisteria, in Algiers, in which my father's shadow built its nest, tracing their gentle smiling images as familiar as the glad apparitions that mingle with the music of our reveries. Of death, we think, our own, yours, mine, his, about the elegance of the ladies of the house all dressed up to greet any visitor who happens by. My mother wears a leopard-print sweater. It crosses my mind that she's hiding the threatening mobile truth of the maculation, which has taken her skin hostage, beneath the artful daubs on the fabric. Or maybe it's an acknowledge-ment of the verdict of whose truth she never breathes a word. I therefore speak loud and clear and soberly for at least two of the deaf. The two sisters were forever congratulating each other on the one's superiority over the other, acknowledged and highlighted, to Éri the attributes of haute couture, the dress that crosses the centuries from Balzac to Proust, for all the art's – and hence love's – gold is present in these marvels of skill and embroidered velvet, to Ève the curiosity, the common sense of common sense, the astonishment polished up anew each morning, all those qualities regularly exercised that constitute the force of her philosophy, even when this latter is surreptitiously attacked by Deafness.

– *Death*, I say: la *mort*. Nope, don't know that either, my mother says. And she throws the door wide to the news of the world . . . . Killed, was he?

I hesitate. Was he killed? In a way he was killed, but they didn't take his death away from him, I say, my mother perches on the edge of the chair, and in the look my mother fixes on the uncertain footsteps of my words I see her entering the room in the Athens prison, this reminds me of the room in Barberousse Prison, she thinks, he was condemned to death, I say, did he have a trial? my mother replies. This for her is familiar ground. They can always find something to accuse good people of. Socrates, that was in Greece, no? They had some dictators who got assassinated too late. When I tell my mother what Plato who, being ill, wasn't there, recounted of what Phaedo, who, all the more affected as he himself had been a prisoner once, before being set free and converting to philosophy, told him of the longest, the most detailed, and finally the most unbelievable tale in the whole history of philosophers and philosophy – lucky for him there was someone who admired him who remembered to write it all down at such a time, says my mother – naturally I condense the whole scene, it resembles a spherical theater which spins slowly within another theatrical sphere, so that when my mother glimpses the entrance to the room in which Socrates explains himself to his friends she simultaneously glimpses scenes in prisons she herself has had occasion to live in or to visit. Her eyes widen, I recognize the extraordinary effect of sympathy. It's as if her entire soul expanded to make room for these scenes, which Phaedo passes on, still steaming, still shuddering with contending emotions, to Plato, scenes in which everyone has Socrates' heart and legs, painful to begin with then dilated all the more so as a moment of relief fol- lows on a twinge sharp enough to elicit a yelp of pain, with the result that – I am greatly struck by this, moved – her eyes, damp, dark, endowed with lateral vision, soft and gaping like the eyes of cows, bulge, so that all I see are those big eyes, I forget everything, and I speak to the eyes of my mother. They are all of her. When I arrive at the hemlock – I make it brief.

(I can't tell my mother that I never read about the last

moments of the last day without tears coming to my eyes just at the paragraph where Socrates is going to see to the washing of his body and getting everything ready so that the others will have as little bother as possible with his corpse, and maybe too because he thinks that these youngsters who will tidy up, after, won't do it with his own sense of perfection, this thought nags at him, and all the thoughts that flutter over the unthinkable thought of being dead, he's careful not to talk about this, it's a flock of butterflies one must no longer heed)

– Soon it will be hemlock time I say.

I hear myself, I see myself. I can see Socrates, my mother. I say: *Hemlock*. I lift the word up to the light. It has a censer-like beauty.

– That's awful!

My mother's face, regretful, pale corolla, eyes of a bull.

– *Brief let me be*, says the ghost of the tale. I am thinking of nightfall. I write to nightfall.

He wasn't smart enough to flee such a death. Yet another one, she thinks. Not smart enough, despite his extraordinary intelligence. Yourfather too, such stupidity. Is it inevitable?

I think: I think of my mother's sun. Of her luminosity. Of the light in her eyes grown wide with the hospitality she makes room for inside herself, and which manifests itself so visibly. Believe me. It must be believed: Socrates died yesterday, I see it in my mother's face. Socrates: dead only yesterday. I mean: for my mother Socrates has just died. And now, I wonder, how to translate all this? All this: all this relivedsurrection of Socrates dying again yesterday in my mother, by my mother. She thinks he shouldn't have let them put him to death. I don't regret my prison days says my mother. But one doesn't need to linger.

When I tell my mother that I think Socrates did not believe Socrates should run away, I mean he had no means, no reason to flee, he thought he would live again I say

– That's awful! my mother exclaims. She relives. She relives all the misery, the day the sun, the prison's big room, it was a very fine day yesterday. She is very stirred up. Another piece of stupidity. Hard to believe. He too has a flaw. –He believed the soul was immortal, I say. – Or so he hoped. She wants to make excuses for him, I muse. And so do I, suddenly I waver, I feel dissociated, I no longer clearly know whether I want to justify Socrates that is whether I side with him sincerely, or from force of habit, cliché, lack of imagination, out of laziness and negligence or out of conviction, or whether I go along with my mother whom I've never, up to now, gone along with. Am I with Socrates or with my mother? Where am I? Here's what happens next: all of a sudden the scene revolves on itself, with all the added scenes, it describes a half-circle and *it comes back in reality.* How powerful, close, full of colors is reality, this is my mother's doing. Her glossy bull's eyes, stern and infinitely practical. Everything must be considered. My mother too, true, would like to be on Socrates' side, at least as far as possible, that is as long as he is still alive, as long as things can still be talked about in prison.

Such a fine day. The winds are blue. Down in the harbor the fishermen embark. The cats aren't stupid, they remain alongside, near the quay, stretched out on the coils of rope. All this is visible from the window of the prison. My mother is in the scene. Her scene. Even there, at such an hour. Along comes the meal cart. –You see, yet another inadequate gesture. This guard, not a bad guy, the one who dishes it all up, the poison with the rest. If I were in his shoes, says my mother, I'd *push*, not *pull.* The cart. Common sense dictates one should exert oneself in the right direction. It's a matter of physics, ethics, politics. A lost cause. All my life I've wanted to lend a hand says my mother, but mortals aren't the sort to take a helping hand. Poor Socrates, right to the last he's giving advice. What's the point, asks my mother. You have a wise mother, but with a message nobody pays any attention to, says my mother. I can't believe it. I myself catch myself giving in much too easily. As if I were, fast asleep, in a dream, beside Socrates, on Socrates' side, against myself, and at the same time, foragainst, Socrates, mama, me bewitched by myself, mama holds out her helping hand, I'm about to grasp it, exit this boat that is very much like a cage, leap onto the bank, saved at the last minute, when I remember I left my black briefcase with all my papers in the hold, I go back down, and hear my mother's voice up there cheering me on: that's it you already have one monkey on your shoulders and another on your back. When I get back to my mother, she hasn't lost all hope of some kind of salvation for Socrates. – Fine, the time has come. Time for the poison. My mother sighs. – But no, the sun is not yet down. Look. I give her Plato's article to read. Now the sun halts for a moment. She reads, slowly, she heaves a sigh. Her immortal soul is in the little room. Socrates seated. My mother seated. Right up close. She's wearing beige trousers. I note: two tiny bloodspots on the thigh. She's wearing a beige and coral striped blouse. She holds Phaedo-signed-Plato's story, now she reads now she sees, I watch her left hand, the one that spilled blood on her trousers. One big purple blotch masked by gauze and a bandage. It's already healed says my mother. A sore several fingers wide. I follow the scent of the wound, like the ghostly guard dog I am. There are two kinds of wisdom. At least. The one my mother turns toward Socrates. The other kind, the kind that she turns toward herself, is a doubtful wisdom in my view, I don't trust it, this self-assurance with regard to which I have licit or illicit doubts illegitimate or not. But I side with my doubts. The hemlock comes fast I tell myself. I spy, I creep, I groan. What time is it? asks Socrates. As you see, says Crito. The sun is about to set says Socrates. Because he took a long time in his bath, and not one two three like me thinks my mother, but I guess that's how men are, next come the orphans, his children his disciples, the cousins, the whole family is there, which is good and not good. But, says Crito, *the sun*, if I'm not mistaken, *is still* on the mountains and *it has not finished going down*, says Crito, or so the story has it, for Socrates the sun is already down the same sun is not yet down, nobody dares affirm that, I go down like the sun says Socrates, it's a present that can take some time, but nobody dares contradict the sun, it is still on the mountains says the story's delegate, but *only if I am not mistaken*, however everyone knows he is mistaken since Crito is not Crito in person, but Phaedo's lieutenant, Phaedo who was himself sent by Plato to Socrates' death, for no one wants to be there, but no one can not want to be present at an event as terrifying as the setting of the Sun.

"There's still time" says the very old voice of my mother far, far away, she is phoning from Athens, and all the pain of the world slips into this sentence of unfathomable harshness. There's still time we say, Phaedo Plato my mother, we who tremble, and don't know what this phrase, *eti gar egkorei*, has in store for us and no one will ever be capable of translating its promise, for if it is still allowed, oh this *still* – this *encore* – the voice cracks, oh this *encore* still allowed and already only still allowed, it is therefore not allowed except still. – Where does this thing stop? asks the Old Voice, consonants nibbled by rust. Poor man, I think it's really awful. Doing away with a man like Socrates. She takes a deep breath and says: it's appalling. I can translate this breath which has trouble forcing its way out under the striped blouse: it's the breath of sorrow blocked by a pocket of dried-up tears. With her bandaged hand she would grip Socrates' hand. What a fate. Old Voice old divinity comes goes from Athens, flutters still, it is still still now, there are still people they execute this way. And the person who did away with him, the king, the government, are they dead too? Soon, they must have killed each other. She stares straight ahead: centuries and centuries of injustice. Pause. More centuries. Would there be another kind of century? Pause. No, none. So she comes back. She sits down. Slowly she closes her wide eyelids. She sees Socrates lying on the mattress. Her nose grows longer, as if she were looking with her nose as well, but it's the weight of her sorrow.

– I think he should have resisted, but I see he didn't. That man should not have accepted death. (*Pause.*) Because after death, says my mother, he *couldn't possibly believe* there was anything else. To have drunk that poison! And his friends? And his wife? Xanthippe, they talk about her in Germany. She was such a shrew. *That* Xanthippe they call her. I can't believe that's why he went along with it. Maybe it's in my dictionary. She looks it up. She finds two words at X. One Xant(h)ippe. With or without an h. And xylograph. Her satisfaction is mixed.

– Is it over yet? – No, I say. There's one more page. Before the end. He still had one last thing to say to his friends. Just when my mother was about to leave. Right up to the last minute one can still do something stupid.

– I hope he didn't forgive his assassin. Not forgiving, what's more, is not the same as being vindictive, vengeance like forgiveness is excessive. One must find the right distance. Neither iron pot nor clay pot. As far as that goes Socrates and my mother are pretty much of one mind.

– Have you heard of Asclepius? I say.

Going from my mother to Socrates, I become aware that I have hope too. Traipsing after my mother I go from hope to hope, each time one hope is lost she comes up with another that carries her a little further on, and so she will never have sunk into despair. Guess what his last words are? I say. Already he was icy cold to the very pit of his belly, therefore what remained was just time to say one last thing to his friends. So my mother bends over, her immense little face becomes one ear, straining, like a hand that wants to touch, receive, not lose some terribly precious words, and who fears a blow from the contrary cousin – Deafness – she is ready, she has her midwife's face that watches for the last push and the first cry, and soberly, precisely, body to body with the patient, without any confusion, she welcomes: what comes out of the mouth of Socrates. It's the first such delivery. So Socrates lifts the sheet that shrouds his face and to my mother he says: We owe a cock to Asclepius. Will you remember to pay my debt? – Consider it done. – You see, he was an honest man. He didn't leave with the bill. On the other hand he submitted to the judgment of those idiots. I think he should have given them the slip. He should have done it for the others because everything he said was worth hearing. His good friends should have *foh*rced him to take flight. What I think says my mother: his disciples should have saved him. They tell him: one more hour, there's still time. In the end that's the way it goes. I am unable to accept *that*. She doesn't accept. And all these great friends of his weeping, Socrates the one who doesn't weep. Like her. She stares straight ahead and decidedly he could have saved his skin. – The world's a big place, right? Couldn't he find a boat, go away, with some friends? They don't want a helping hand. She folds her hands in her lap. She is sitting with the body. Me, I would have given them the slip. It takes more courage to run away than to submit. There are limits to submission. His wisdom was the tranquil kind. He should have been a rebel. Especially since he was still young. I see he has two small children. Yourfather too. My father too –

In my opinion: there's no such thing as friends. The day I had to leave, I just had time to pack a bag, I was to take a plane if there was one, the last day in Algiers, the sun going down, *nobody* lent me a hand. I call Dr L. I say: I am *foh*rced to leave.

On the last plane. Ah! I can't I have a sore throat. Mr Charles: I can't. My wife is leaving tomorrow. Mr Chesnais: I left my car with a cousin in France he was dead. Raoul: he had some kind of story with his mother once she was dead. I must sleep with my mother first. There were lots of people around me. All the same. Cowards. Incredible. She bursts out laughing. The next day when I got here, when I got to your place I had a good laugh. Only, I didn't even get to see Algiers for the last time. That's *my* wisdom.

His wisdom dictated that he go along with *That*. He didn't look for the *helicopter* to take him away. She is pleased to have come up with *helicopter* because it's Greek. Ah! That Socrates. This *really* upsets me. *Really.* The way that poor Socrates thought he was proving something by not saving himself, he hadn't a hope in the world of saving anything at all. Why do you give me such dreadful things to read? I can't agree. Even the cock. I see he says: *we owe* a cock. Not me. I don't think *he* owes any cocks to anybody. Hemlock! That's really antique. It's out of date. Now it's electricity, which doesn't always work. Hemlock, *Ciguë* that is, do you write that with a *c*? I still have my classic dictionary published in Paris German–French. She doesn't find it. Is it written with a *y*? – With *i*, I say. *Ci* like Cixous. – No it's not there. There's *Cicade*. – Are you looking in German? – It's an antiquity. I have another book that's also an antique.

Der Glückel von Hameln 1623–1719. It's been around for a while. 1719. Ninety-five years old can you believe? They were Germans, Jews from Hamburg. A very interesting life, difficult. The seventeenth-century Jews were looked down on. Always being accused of corruption. People were always getting mad at them if they behaved themselves, especially since they were all Protestants or Catholics. They were always getting expelled. This Glückel wrote the history of the seventeenth-century Hamburg Jews. She wrote German

86

with Hebrew letters. Her son donated his papers written by his mother. People bought this book for the quality of its wisdom. Who bought it for me later on? *Rosi Klein*, it's marked. That's my mother. *1914 Berlin.* With her finger she follows. This is a book one always reads for the first time. – The book is like you, I say. A big volume, orderly, hefty and its skin torn, a canvas that time's teeth shred. – It was a handsome book says my mother, it must have been expensive. Now I'm going to do the beans, says my mother. Her cheery voice. The beans as if by a leguminous elevator bring the shades of the dead right up to our door.

– Whereas with his hemlock that he fohrced himself to glorify he didn't save a single soul, poor Socrates.

It is a plant that resembles wild chervil, with a thick stalk, smooth but with red or dark blotches, the fruit small, globular. Some decree, whose secret we don't know, says it grows among ruins. This makes me dream. *Conium maculatum.* Plants that live on ruins. Ruins that nourish big toxic chervil plants. The servant, who knows what he is talking about, says one must drink just enough for the dose to be mortal. Neither more nor less. I write the word *hemlock* on a loose sheet of paper.

The book "here" is called Hemlock *in the meantime.*

While I write, I may forget to weep. In the same way, inexplicably, unforeseeably, I may be unable to hold back tears. The moment of tears comes. Socrates' good friends weep, each according to his memory and his emotion, the one a trickle the other torrents, all of them as Socrates drinks down the tears of the hemlock, on these tears I too weep, I wander among all those who know not why they weep. Because he is already dead says Phaedo that is Crito, the alreadydead person speaks to us, no, the dead person still speaks to us, he is living, the invisible is everywhere, it envelops each word in a scrap of paper each smile in a gauze of notyetstill, this butterfly wing membrane, oh notmuchtime, a slow dagger, feather, scales of time that fall from my eyes. – Don't cry, says Socrates. All the same you are incredible! I rebel. Utterly. Against me, you, him, her, that, already not yet too soon still a moment soon later too late, and what to say of After? And what to say of Before?

– *Before*, says my mother – she glances down at her young woman trousers, in her outfit she's forty years old – I'd go shopping with Éri, I'd go to the market, we'd rummage around, we bought everything that way, I watch them rummage in the street vendors' stalls, excited, knowledgeable, hen birds deftly feathering their refugee nest, the refugees they will have been from 1935 right to the end, makers of light, practical hiding places, unflagging, buying time and all the rest, dresses, trousers, life, strength, victory, I can still see their luxuries, *I got it for a song*, says my mother, beaming so early in the morning oblivious of time's claws, pride wells up in my mother today as in the days of Osnabrück or Socrates, a living earned, to this satisfaction add that of the melt-in-the-mouth expression, a tidbit of French – *pour une bouchée de pain* – it too turned up among the riches of the jumble sale – *for a song* – crowning glory, the title of the trousers, of the dress, I look at the pair of trousers found by Ève bearing Éri's stamp of approval she's the one who takes the part of Minos in the market's secret scenes, I see all these shadows of beings, shapes that will turn into bodies or rags, pressing together on the verge of wretchedness, their animal charms promised to salvation or to death still beckon modestly from under the cut-price labels. All it took to fish up this blouse, this jacket from a jumble of mortal remains was the flick of an artist's wrist. And this magic, it's my mother led by my aunt who makes it happen. Off they go to Hell, on Friday, because Saturdays there are too many people. Twentieth-century history can be read in the huge wicker carryalls. Sitting alongside my mother's trousers, I hear the World speaking and by the light of my mother I see Homer, Dante, Balzac, Proust, my mother, my aunt, all bent over the same basketful of the splendors and dreams of all the condemned who have managed to give the "king, that assassin" the slip says my mother. For she's always seen the assassin coming, never has she allowed herself to be fooled by his kingly appearance, and similarly, she on her part has always kept a healthy distance between herself and all kings. That for her is the song, the *bouchée de pain*. Which reminds me of that extraordinary dress the white one with a diamond pattern made in Germany with pockets. That's how Germany was once lost and she and Éri bought it back at the market. – I could change three times a day with all the clothes I have, says my mother. And I don't wear dresses. She says this on July 7, 2007. She doesn't, I notice, say: I don't wear dresses any more. This would constitute an unacceptable acceptance of the pemphigoid fatality, the foreign body that colonizes and turns her skin against her. When my sober mother says: I don't wear dresses, she pits herself with her faithful weapons against fate's monstrous gesticulations. I don't wear dresses, that scrap of fabric so discreet on the mouth of the wound that the unruly monster is cowed. – "Misfortune is hard but lighter to those who accept it" as your friend Montaigne says, says my mother. I, however, do not accept just any kind of accepting. Only up to a point.

Before has barged into the house. Before, *Before* didn't get a seat at the table so often, so full of shiny new aplomb and yet so bossy, in my mother's speeches, in the bedroom, in the kitchen. When *Before* pops out of my mother's mouth, like a word that's taking command, I try to act as if I didn't hear it, and now I too, copying my mother, bow to the adversary as little as I can. But at bottom, *Before* goes straight to my heart. Uncouth, to my eyes, it's what I see, when, having entered my mother's room without her hearing me, for Deafness distracts and exposes her, I find her still in her underwear, busy taking stock of the ravaged terrain. I can't not steal up on the surface, naked with dissimulation, of my mother, in a state that she alone in the world has the ability to analyze, *Before*, I mean, the mysterious, deft arrangements that allow her to hide the damage from my inspection. For as a woman arrays herself beyond what is imaginable in order to shine in the eyes of her lover, finding ways to erase wrinkles, smooth folds, all this without the use of cosmetics, through the marvelous work of love, so my mother primps for me, rendering smooth, at least for a fraction of a second, the skin on her chest that I'd thought spared right up until this morning when, taking her by surprise, I discovered the crimps, the blood-veined furrows she manages by who knows what genius of the bosom to keep out of sight when I am around. *Before*, says my mother. And these two stressed syllables have something gentle and German. *Before* must have begun to glimmer in the privacy of my mother's thoughts at the beginning of the month of January 2007. I remember it was February I noticed that *Before*, which came and went intermittently, always with the quaver of a voice that calls, fluttering at an invisible windowpane, had become, according to the discreet wish of my mother, a sort of name for the ellipsis of Éri. Thanks to *Before* and as *Before* my mother started to take Éri shopping again, not long "After." Here's how: when she goes to the market, she acts just like *Before*, brandishing her cane she runs from stall to stall with Éri at her heels, but replaced mostly by my brother, unless it's me. Since she never turns back, she never doubts that Éri is still shadowing her.

COUSIN DEAFNESS

Catching the sea in a net is my obsession, my fixation, I'm vaguely aware of the folly of the undertaking, but it won't be bossed around, this idea, I spin and I weave I weave mama in and so it goes the nights are especially difficult I work so hard I sleep like a Titan.

According to my mother the heroine of my books has nothing to do with her, besides a book without doors or walls hasn't any "key" just life's hustle-bustle –aside from the famous little key-to-nothing we keep safe in the mauve and white porcelain candy dish because it has the occult charms of an orphan.

According to my mother our first task is to make sure the car is running. It has been hibernating for the past year in the garage.

My mother takes charge of the operation. Under her orders and the pocket lamp I re-install the battery. This is hard. I can still see her at the wheel of the Renault saying only she can get it going in one shot. About this she is mistaken.

But I stop myself from contradicting what is the source of her pride. One turn of the starter. And all her campaigns are up and running, en route for their victories.

I get the car started. In her excitement my mother sees herself at the wheel. She jingles the keys. Her cane puts her in her place. When I back out of the garage she imagines she'd do this better. Which doesn't keep her from congratulating herself on the endurance of the old car. Congratulating the old dame on her endurance. Bliss.

Melancholy eats at my heart not hers.

I've done a lot of time, her thoughts are thinking, I've given my good fortune a helping hand. The rest of them run out of gas before ninety-five. So long as the car is working something of my mother at the wheel goes on driving in my stead. – The day this car stops running, she says. She lets the sentence dangle, because today it works. I merely drive, she makes the signals. I take the car for a spin. The old girl jingles, wavers, reacts so lethargically I have to slow down: the brakes are on their last legs. All goes well. Now when I take the car out, I take it out for my mother and I take my mother the car out. We go for a spin. I bring the car back to my mother. She studies the old mount. – You know you need to wipe her windshield? I was most careful to do so. She notices. Had I not done so, her spin was spoiled, I would objectively have routed her ghost. She sees the gleaming windshield: am I not still at the wheel?

When I come back I hear an unholy racket, Schubert's *Quintet in C Major*. It's that old radio Damart Ladieswear gave her as a bonus. Turn it off! I say. Turn it down! My mother's deafness has got out of hand since Cousin Deafness joined the household. She came along a few years ago, inseparable and totally uneducable. Her influence seeps into all the rooms in the house, on the staircase, it incites my mother to excesses, these digital thunderings, television explosions, for which my mother and her cousin are not responsible. They switch on the crackly old kitchen radio, and soon my mother and her cousin, hearing only a vague burble because everyone speaks too quickly and into their beards, forget all about it. They leave the room. However, left to itself, the machine gets carried away and a conflagration of sound swells until it devours the silence of my study. The door! The radio! I shout. My sentence already dead. Eyes shooting sparks I descend. I bang open and to no purpose the door to my mother's room. For her this is always a pleasure. The door signifies: I come to woo you. She lifts her eyes from her book, the story of a daughter attached to her mother that she detests she doesn't understand a word it must be Japanese because it can't be Chinese. And she is reading! Oh my book, my book, encroached on by the frothing and foaming pack of hounds whose baying my mother doesn't hear. Meanwhile she who delivered me reads on. Turn it down! I shout, and I screech, at the top of my lungs like the quintet: Turn it down! *Baisse!* Next I see her wondering where to find this thing I so frantically demand, whose name she didn't quite catch. – She said *laisse*, Deafness prompts. *A leash* – for what? says my mother. Something to do with the cats? – Maybe she said: *caisse*, Deafness falters. My mother, embarrassed, eyes down. A box, no, that's not it she tells herself, but what to do, ridicule is inevitable when one has an inner cousin who gets everything mixed up. – You don't have your ears? I say outlining the question in front of them slowly. No. She doesn't have her ears. The cousin's fault, the old woman prefers not to be bothered with all those gimmicks and their infernal noise. In secret my mother is on the cousin's side, in public, no. At the same time, in another corner of the secret, she sides with my authority. I too am of two minds. It occurs to me that my mother may take some pleasure of which I'm not aware in her Deafness, I can even imagine a certain voluptuousness in exploring states of soul that reside only in the deeps, maybe my mother now revels in an amphibious life she can't yield to freely for she must think I think that these dives under the family table are unorthodox, I imagine the sensation of transgression that, without using or knowing the word transgression, must have a strongly disquieting savor. It occurs to me that there may be a touch of mischief in these furtive pleasures into which Deafness initiates her, a thought that wouldn't occur to her. I've heard enough! who knows whether she doesn't think that, I might and shall think. But think enough, never. The time has come to think to my heart's content, all day long. I plug my ears and I let myself sink into the mirrory waters of reverie. Maybe she goes to the Thatremindsme Cinema where the show never stops. And to think I cobble myself together a poor prophetic deafness. No matter how much wax one stuffs one's ears with, one still hears the Sirens. Through the wax the quintet or the quartet is devilishly seductive. I'd jump overboard to drown out the music that interrupts my inner music. On the other hand I'm afraid my mother, who has always been an earthly arch-enemy of daydreaming, is going to destroy herself with dives that are contrary to her better nature. Should she follow or resist Deafness's murmur? That Deafness misleads her when she stays at the surface, makes her hear *messie* for *vessie*, messiah for bladder, that's how bad it gets, that Deafness has a twisted mind and is at the root of tantrums, letting my mother think her daughter is guilty of an anti-Semitic slur which I'm not, as a result of a malevolence to which my mother lends herself, this may be disagreeable, but these errors of reading also give rise to much comedy, especially since the family granted the tortuous old cousin the status of fool in Shakespeare's plays. It occurs to me that my antipathy for Deafness, which I fight, which I reprove, might be linked to a painful representation, that I brush aside, of a future when I envision myself not shouting: Turn it down! Turn it off! For by then Deafness will have led her far away from me, out of earshot. But this thought is dispersed by a hoot of laughter from my mother who, seeing me turn off the radio, has suddenly realized what the missing word was.

Later I tell myself when I hear this quintet, I'll see my mother standing in the garage, at noon, just out of bed, still in her bathrobe, already her hands which have gathered into themselves all the strength that has deserted her little body rummaging in the abdomen under the hood, impelled by an urgent desire to check on how "she's doing." Or so I hope. It may also be that I never hear this quintet again, at least by chance. However, only the melody coupled with the surprise will bring back Eurydice.

THE JERK

The jerk, says my mother. The jerk. He saunters down the Allée Samuel Beckett. His method: threats, maybe-maybe-nots, innuendos. A slippery character who knows how to attract attention, or go unnoticed just long enough to pop up again just when one forgets about him. The Jerk, for the first time she gives him a name. Before, no. One spoke of him in vague, general, terms, he was of course the main character of my mother's knowledgeable-insect activities, secret sharer in her meticulous preparations, the being each clause of whose law my mother studies. She says: *The Jerk*, on January 2, 2006. I like it. My mother has a way with words, a je-ne-sais-quoi, a chic. *Chic* is one of my mother's words. I take it. She doesn't know this but somewhere inside her, in the year 1918, a little girl pedals like mad around Strasbourg Cathedral, changing languages at each spin of the wheel. In the front of the church, the *Geschick* kingdom, first destiny, around the corner, on the Synagogue side: chic. Languages speak to her, inspire her, little old Pythia with her eyes banded, she knows

97

not what she says but each word knows a thing or two, her cup brims over and she's none the wiser. Most of the time the words that cross her path make her laugh: their power is beyond her. Now where does that come from? Never would she have said that. Jerk. *Salaud*. A word she's never uttered. "Jerk." She considers it, says it again. Goodness! Did she say that word? It came along. No problem. It suits him. The word fits him – The Jerk – like a glove. Do you know how to say "glove" in German? *Handschuh*. The Jerk has hand shoes that way one doesn't see his claws. Mine are the commentaries. My little Pythia spits the words out. No explanation. Abrupt. She balances her cup of tea. She's setting it down? She flings it at the table. And the cup doesn't shatter. All her gestures stiffened, hard. The cause is the inner armor, an invisible iron in which she has instinctively coated her mind foreseeing The Jerk's dirty tricks. I like it. I make a note of the date. A notch in the alleyway of Time that runs from Denfert to the end. I note the many cards in the deck of the wordplay. The word is foreign many times over. A word foreign to the family like all French vulgarities, whose resources my mother and German grandmother were unaware of, and which, from the days when Germany-resided-in-Algiers, haven't lost their tinge of exoticism. The Jerk is a luxury, a conquest, Jerk is exciting, like the enormous, too big ice cream cones in the Street of the Jews in Oran, where this word was also in the cafés. The jerks are the good-for-nothings says my mother. *Ein Taugenichts, aus dem Leben eines Taugenichts*, nothing good comes of his life, it's innate says my mother. She mulls this over: he's somebody like that brother of Omi's who has defects who has only defects, a born-defective. A lout, that's what he is. The pink Butterfly Japanese pajamas keep time to her rhapsody. She stitches, a litany of jerks. Then there's the last one, a mother-killer the Benjamin who kills himself to kill his mother in one blow, her grandmother I mean Benjamin's mother saw that the last of the sons was the end of everything and that put an end to their story. Meanwhile Uncle Basto I can't say he was a jerk, you couldn't call him honest either, I noticed he lived beyond his means, living beyond one's means of living to my way of thinking this is suspicious, he was a shoe salesman, I don't know the details of his acts. He was still alive after the war. Survived everyone, the men that is. And how about this? he always dressed his three sons exactly the same three times the expense whereas in our house we wore hand-me-downs, they got deported, communists. She sews, one goes from city to city, from life to life – we never called him Solomon, it's too long, he married a woman no one liked, the family never much liking the daughters-in-law this Helma a smart cookie, fingers always in the jam pot. But the last of Omi's five brothers was the crookedest of the lot. Born crooked. The Jerk, I've never used this word before. No reason to. Yourfather ought to have made more use of it. He mustn't have known such people existed, *ein schlechter Mensch* it wouldn't cross his mind. If his life depended on it, which it did. Whereas I myself have always ee-lim-in-ay-ted whatever jerks crossed my path. What's all this jerk business? She thinks it over. Searches. Finds: guess what happened to me? My socks are missing. Yesterday I had four, two blue and two white. This morning only two, one blue and one white. Someone's after my things. – It can only be you I say. I mean the other. – And what's he going to do with *one* blue sock and the other white?

The Jerk she says to avoid saying *whoever's stealing her things*, who walks and hides just so he can pop out at her strolling along the Allée Samuel Beckett. To show all the bad things she thinks about that character and hence about her own state of preparedness. She tells and doesn't tell. So, I tell myself, this is how she sees things. Without any complacency. He who comes is to be *avoided*. I relish this and it saddens me:

it's the first time. That she names him, even, or perhaps above all, by antonomasia, is a way of acknowledging him, admitting that he is on her mind as she is on his, for she thinks that he thinks of her, he gives her the jitters, this troublemaker. From now on The Jerk prowls around us, under the name of enemy. Me and my mother: my mother is me. We know and we know nothing, except the name. Me and my life. My life and my death.

– I'm clean, says my mother. I've had my shower. I'm having my coffee. It is noon.

I like noon; in general it's not The Jerk's time of day. The Jerk's hours are more the wee hours, the darkling surreptitious propitious to plot ones. More than once I've been seen dashing like a madwoman down the Allée Samuel Beckett between nine and ten in the morning. All the hours between midnight and mama, the hours of dirty work. During which I sleep, I head off to dreamland, but I am awake, I hear everything, I fear everything, I believe I hear, I start up, I want to run, *run* cries my heart but my legs stutter, my cats wake up, my real ones, my walkyries, you are asleep Aletheia tells me, you know that I always tell the truth, but still if you must run, if you think the dream is the reality, we'll tumble downstairs with you, to make your legs move, do as we do. I touch the cats, the warmth, I move my legs, they move. I realize I was dreaming. But aren't dreams a quarter of reality? This is unclear. That the dream should occur during sleep doesn't make it less true. Some dreams are premonitory. They warn us. Had we known they were the Premonitory Ones, we'd have heeded them. But such is our fate, we don't know that we'll only know later on. We are the unforewarned forewarned. Like in Shakespeare. They don't forearm us, the premonitory dreams, quite the contrary. They forewarn us askew. The person who might be saved does not receive the dream letter. To Julius Caesar the audience shouts: it's true what the dream announced, don't you see those bastards prowling around behind the beautiful pine trees summer untimely warms? Don't go! – Off I go says the dreamer. He goes to be put to death, it's incomprehensible. It might have been avoided. Is this a premonitory dream? I ask myself. Should I run to my mother? The second part of this cruel circus has already begun. I may have sat through it a hundred times, the pain is as grotesque as ever, artlessly one suffers, without even my shoes! I can't dash off barefoot, in the middle of the night, this has no importance whatsoever, I'm going to hurt myself, it doesn't matter, but run barefoot to the hospital, for already I see the hospital looming, its hold packed with the dying, where I arrive barefoot, with mama in a blanket. And without documents? And therefore without phone. I must turn the light on, find my shoes, that's the first thing. I turn on the light. This of course wakes me up. I note that I dreamt I was dreaming probably a premonitory dream and finally I woke up and I made a note of what I'd just dreamt I was writing that I'd dreamt I was dreaming a premonitory dream, none of which in any way resolves my anguish. Should I dart to my mother's? I can't run over there every time I have a dream. And yet. I was in Rome, who was I? Someone who knew they were going to be killed. Funny, that didn't stop me having a strong feeling of nostalgia, to find myself in those streets, around noon, especially because underfoot my sandals recognized the density of the cobbles, the unevenness of those beautiful blocks of stone one beside the other, joined and disjointed in their intervals by that red earth that mixes the beginning of life with what will be ruins, in other words, survival. We were going to die and I reveled in the beauty, for each of us mortal, just as in Algeria when I was small and sure we were going to die, I reveled at noon in the immortality of us all, we the human readers and magicians of ruins, for at the same hour before death, when I felt my intolerable lack of power to annul the verdict, reacting with a stubborn determination to at least delay the moment as long as possible at least in the case of mama, the wellspring that is of my philosophy, I savored once again Shakespeare's magnificent emotion when he visited Rome in a dream as if he were there in reality, it was as if this dream's emotion remained on the unbelievably smooth skin of the big eternal stones of the alley, I sat down on a tomb, I laid my palms on its face, one stone over from me I could clearly make out Stendhal, alive, sitting in white trousers writing in a moleskin notebook, I saw it distinctly, only he I told myself really sat on these stones, you can tell, it is true I don't *see* Shakespeare, or Balzac, places keep, I told myself, all one needs is to find oneself in Rome,

  – I've made my bed already.
  I've come downstairs to my mother. I'm back.
  Blackcurrant and rhubarb, says my mother. How are things upstairs my darling? – Upstairs is a never-ending battle, I say. – Against whom? Yourself? Take a break. – Who's Black Current and Rhubarb? I ask. For me they are the names of the little horses that so delight Stendhal. – Jam, says my mother. She raps the table with her spoon. – There are many kinds of ghosts, I say. You are my cock. This summer the ghosts are winning, my cock gets up later and later, the sun doesn't come out much, it's high noon on the clock when the tragic troop at last flees my study. Quick as a wink enter Cock, Black Current, Rhubarb, a change of style. My opera is parataxical. – You need your little mother says my July 10 mother. I won't say your little turd, no. You need an *object* to cajole and love. The spoon emphasizes the word *object*. *Object*.
  – You said *Object*, I say. – I didn't *say* that. It popped up. It's a word I've never used. *Object* is a word from the old scholastics, a word from philosophy's word hoard. On the one hand

this Jerk takes her socks. On the other *he* provides her with words not her style. I myself never use the word *object* in front of my mother, I address her in her language, and I only philosophize in my study with my books or phone. You'd think my mother had been philosophized. That the absent still be among us, that the Invisible be peopled, I myself have not the slightest doubt. But my mother, who has principles, has not in sixty years received a single visit from my father, an event without a hope of happening for her, a person untroubled by doubt, for whom everything that is is final, my mother for the insubstantial naturally skittish and somewhat umbrageous beings, I put myself in their shoes, is an insurmountable barrier.

I'm the one who has just been rereading *Three Essays on the Theory of Sexuality* up there, first in French then in German, then *Me – Psychoanalysis*, and I admit I thought of my mother seeing Jacques Derrida's face flicker with the quick and almost unreadable shadow of that familiar wry look that appears in the corner of a phrase in which he has taken advantage of his equivocal French to throw the reader off balance, for my mother could have uttered one of the two phrases concealed in the words Me – psychoanalysis, not the phrase with two subjects obviously, the other. I could what's more picture my mother, psychoanalysis, uttering me – psychoanalysis, with various intonations, letting me decide whether she meant: Me – psychoanalysis, I know nothing about it, or, me – psychoanalysis, I can do without. Because Me – Psychoanalysis, that she wouldn't of course say. She would have neither the narcissistic resources nor the rhetorical reserves, nor the deftness, nor the surreptitious legitimacy which is the stealer of fire's genius. I spent an ageless, timeless moment up there in the company of my mother and Jacques Derrida without feeling, during that conversation come from another reality, any difference of kind between the people my imagination summoned up around a phrase and as usual everything went swimmingly between "yourmother" as he says, "myboy" as she says, and my enchanted silence. – How would you translate that? *Ich – und die Psychanalyse* that's two things, says my mother. Let me tell you something: *Me?* What does *me* mean? It's not very different from psychoanalysis. You must be a good subject for the psychoanalysts. Not me. I've never paid much attention to my psyche. I live *day to day*. No need of a *me* for that. And the psychology of others – what can you do about that? To each his madness. Give them a piece of advice, they don't take it, they head straight for disaster. Right after that I relived an abridged version of summer 2001. And right after that I sought *The Interpretation of Dreams* on my shelves, prompted by a feeling of necessity I always trust like a prophet whose blindness doesn't stop him finding the door his god on the all-powerful phone told him to take. I didn't know what I'd find but doubt I did not. It's as if this Telepathy who was once the ghostly friend of my friend Jacques Derrida, but whom I don't believe I've ever met in person, whom I've heard about, of course, but who has always for me been one of those characters some societies make much of, a great lady of reference, I pictured her, without much sympathy, as someone like the Duchess of Guermantes (whom I've never met either strictly speaking, while having met her dozens of times, and this, I must confess, is doubtless my own doing, owing to my lack of attraction, in other words because of the opposite feeling, a slight mistrust I've never felt compelled to analyze) or perhaps like the Princess of Cadignan, which isn't her name, and in whom, anonymous witnesses claim, is *buried* an otherwise famous duchess, become a stranger under the princess, that is under her name, and who is therefore more than one, of whom we can say she forever leads a double life, and whom the society of Saint-Germain-des-Prés, like all psychoanalytical societies, respectfully and discreetly protects, as befits one of her name, without explanation, it's as if this Telepathy had behind my back invited herself up earlier as I was leafing through *The Interpretation of Dreams*, and at the same moment my mother, who, left to her own devices, would never have read Freud, had perhaps had the visit of this same Telepathy who says the same thing to two minds separated by time and space. On that day when, without giving it a second thought, I opened the *Traumdeutung* door, I took the back door, led as always by Blindness that knows, and starting with the last page which I thus make the first I find Freud – I take him by surprise I suppose because I enter in his back – *en tête-à-tête*. They don't hear me. They say, as if they were finishing up, or perhaps as if he were ending up as two, by being two, more or less this, which I jot down, as if for a dream that is fading:

> *Can dreams, then, predict the future?*
> *– Out of the question. It would be truer to say: dreams reveal the past. For they are rooted in the past.*
> *– Surely the old belief in prophetic dreams is not wholly false. Dreams lead us into the future, by showing us our wishes fulfilled; but this future, which the dreamer pictures as present, is shaped by his indestructible desire, into an image of the past.*

At that moment, I have an overwhelming feeling of happiness. I have just discovered that I am, through an incredible stroke of luck, *in* the Dream of the world of Dreams, of which I've so often heard the great dreamers speak but where I've never yet set foot. And I saw. More precisely: I saw them. The lords of dreams. All those whom one doesn't see and who are not named. I see them still. They call out to one another, from dream to dream, one from his automobile, another on his sailboat, another on the staircase. Socrates is talking to Freud, Derrida to Socrates, Derrida asks Socrates if dreams foretell the future and Freud prepares to answer him, perhaps at the same moment, for all these lords are talking to one another as well as answering *dubitatively*, doubt is the one certainty, what is certain is the eternal question: *and you, do you know what the future holds for you?* But they don't expect an answer, sharing the uncertainty is nonetheless a pleasure, at times, I note, they address each other as old friends, as if it is to themselves they speak, at other times they speak more formally, as if they were addressing themselves as strangers, this conversation is in duration brief, endless in space, I am deeply moved by the proximity of the great separated, the gentle, courteous way they visit with each other over secular distances, each, I feel, feeling himself recalled, in the other, to himself, so often were they wont to dream of the others' dreams that something of them remains – a shore –

where

no one doubts

there may be

there – have

– yet to be seen –

come back

each expects –

– each expects Who-is-death, my friend J.D. says

That depends

on the date, the place, the bus stop, my health, the shore, on the state of the ties, time and tides, the logbook, the lip of the dock we draw alongside, where we await one another, where as I walk the marshlands of Elysium with my brother at my side I glimpse shining over there on the screen of pearl-grey sky the silhouettes of those within me who play on Lethe's quay.

– I love this place's wildness says mybrother.

– Lucky you're here I say, otherwise I'd wake up. I'm discouraged by some of the dreams snaking along this rough track, dotted with poisonous thistles, that skirts the last cliff of the world.

– You know when the theory starts, says mybrother, there's no end in sight. Any further and you find yourself in brambles and scrub.

As if he'd read my thoughts. I take my little notebook from my pocket. I note that the notebook is the only object that stays with me whether I am in the world of the waking or that of dreams. Whence in its pages my two styles of writing. I jot all this in the Pentateuque III notebook. I write: a day of revenants: my brother returns – since he returns along with my friend J.D. something of the latter passes into the former. One of J.D.'s sentences, which I know well from having heard him say it a dozen times, suddenly in the mouth of my brother. But it's wholly my brother's, the affect, the timber, the intonation are my brother's, with the result that this phrase here has an entirely different meaning from J.D.'s anxious and melancholy one. To myself: insert somewhere in the "Jerk" chapter. A chapter in which my mother, who is the main character, is invaded by a throng of Visitors, perhaps because of the date (July 15). I write down: I must think about this society within me in which my living my dead, my gods with their long and short lives live side by side, with my mother in their midst – I don't know where to put that –

Perhaps the motif that comes back most frequently in the book, as strongly or more so than the ave
future of mama
is the motif – as it happens by her prohibited –
of revenants.

She doesn't believe in them. Doesn't believe that Éri, Ève's other half, who departed on December 31, might next year come back.

I feel as if my visitors are wearing her out
(Noted July 16, inserted later)

I come back to my brother.
– A cock, I say. – A cock? – I thought I heard a cock crow.
What is so poignant about the cock's crowing is that can be
heard from dozens of kilometers away, across seas and forests.
– Do you hear it? – I don't hear it any more. – Maybe that
was its last cry says my brother.
– Doyouremember papa's white rooster? I say. There was
also *Le Coq*, his songbook. Whatever has happened to it? We
can go no further, says my brother. We have to turn back.
We come back.

When Freud reaches the last page of his book, he doesn't
know, he doesn't see the end coming. He draws himself up
on the tormented ground of his lecture on the unconscious
when out of the blue – *Cock!* I see him leap off the book in
motion like a fiancé come to say goodbye, who thought he
had a quarter of an hour left before the train's departure. Did
he have time for one last kiss? All of a sudden, in less than no
time, he can feel himself breathing in the day's odor. The bell
is going to ring, the sun, the end is near. On his tongue he feels
the anxious saliva that spurts from under Hamlet-the-ghost's
helmet when his apocalyptic nose gets wind of the scene that
announces *mourning*, the hour at the end of the night that
ushers in the death of dreams, and day's livery. No time *to lose*.
Everything is about to happen, he knows, hackles rising. I who
wanted, he regrets, he hopes, to try to stop believing that I'll
never believe. I'll never be able to believe. Finished! says the
book. Just three more lines! he pleads. The ghost begs him in
English for a reprieve. *Brief, let me be!* But as if he suspected

time which judges to be German, or to expect Freud to speak in his own language, with all the force of persuasion he can muster he makes what he in his theoretical writings calls "a magic wish." "*Ein Brief soll ich werden.*" And that's what happens: he becomes a letter. And what a letter! A big sheet of paper on which *he doesn't see* that he himself has written endless accounts of dreams. With a firm, quick hand he traces, as a medium would, striding along the shore, the question that has been seeking him from the very first page, five hundred and twenty-seven nights ago. Finally what he would have liked to know was if, in the end, dreams foretell the future, just then Socrates, is this Socrates' dream or his own, wakes, having received, or because he has received, the news of the end, and the fact that this is a woman, beautiful, tall, white and black, looking at them with her big eyes as tenderly still as a bottomless pond, untroubled by the impurity of any thought, fills both Socrates and Freud with happiness. Not a word, just a vision. All this takes place *at the moment* Freud is about to say: *Can dreams*, but as his time is up he wakes up quick saying:

"There's no time to lose."

Here the book is called the Ave of my mother.

– How's the book coming along? my brother asks.

It goes, it comes, it escapes again. There's always a ghost page

– *The cock* always says: I'm the boss here, says my mother. He summons all the hens. *Kikeriki*, cockadoodle-do, the cock doesn't crow the same in German and in French. I'm going to sweep all this up. Did I wake you clanking my spurs?

At this moment the "ghosts" are lighter than the crumbs my mother sends with one swipe of her hand into the shadow of the table.

What would the ghosts do without names? There are hours, days like today, I tell myself, when it's so beautiful, the whole earth is clothed in light, there's no limit, no shadow, no immediate threat. Everything is growing. No one can lose their temper, ulterior motives stay in their caves. I "recognize" such times, I've alreadyseen their endless transparence, I've alreadyloved them, this blue verging on white kind of weather, from another time. Let what may happen. If it happens during the crystal time *nothing bad can come of it*. I see my mother: I see her truly. I see my mother. The cats see me see my mother. I see my cats see me see my mother. With their time-colored eyes they gaze at the scene. They too want to be part of the illumination. I look at Aletheia, and I hum: How pretty you are Aletheia! Right away she rolls over, given. Philia waits. I hum: How pretty you are Philia! Philia rolls over on her night back and her night is unveiled. – You are their nurse mother, says my mother. Now I'm going to do The Dishes.

Me – death, says my mother,

I want to paint her voice, photograph it in depth, the voices she has, her voice is no longer in her voice, her voice projected, strong, rude, soberly imperious in the house, her voice of the North toward the South, cold then lukewarm, yields to other voices, hoarse, grating, uncertain, they try, back off, limp in her throat, huff and puff, almost all the inflections change, the only ones that resist, spared by the storm, a few words, determined not to give up. The most victorious is Allô. Allooôô! Mama's rallying cry. Then come: life, death, mydaughter, mycoffee. Not to forget: *hüniquement*, hueniquely. With the accent on the first syllable. And: you, *tu*. *Tu*, high-pitched, drawn-out, with its diphthong.

Me – death

disappearance, *verschallen*, *hinscheiden*, *ausgehen*, *erlöschen* in French I can't translate, *der Tod*, it's all the same thing.

– I didn't ask you to talk about that I say

A sentence goes past: "Do you think about Éri?" I let it go by. I think of Éri, that part, the other part of Ève, a whole life and never said *we*. Two sisters, that is, two towers, two nations, two goats, two hemispheres, two solitudes, one memory. Ève's Solitude changed starting on the first of January. It was missing Éri's earthly Solitude.

– The only picture I have of it is you're lying down, you've stopped breathing, you're cold, it's not interesting.

I go along with this, who knows why.

I want to paint the song of her silence, as she follows life with her eyes, the constant struggle, from her bed, in the old days her mother's bed, in order to feed herself and defend herself and to keep up with the group it's dreadful what's going on in Lebanon when I think such a beautiful country they've managed to ruin it with their wars when she thinks of animals the shepherds especially it can't be easy they are attached to their sheep to each his wolves after all, I am agnostic, in God's presence I am a sheep, he is always bigger than we are, I want to paint the daily song of my mother thinking great frescos of silence, The Jerk, this Death.

Death, who is Death, this poor long-dead God. A pause. The only one who's eternal and he's dead. A pause. Then her voice gets up, it's late, but not too, the world has gone away, she's still here, the peonies are holding on, "the peonies are flourishing" the voice says every year they do better, they outdo themselves, the voice clings to the peonies, grows more affirmative, is pleased. The tale that remakes the world in Ève's image starts up again: "First of all I'm going to go to the kitchen and make my coffee, take down my tray and my board to cut the bread. I'll take my own-cup-not-the-mug the knife and the long-handled spoon and the short spoon I'll arrange whatever has dried overnight on the tea trolley I bought in St-Ouen in 1960 there was a trolley factory and I never found it again. Next I'll protect it with a cloth the one with a little bird on it – that Éri and I once bought" – here there's a slight pause in the narration that will draw its thread out verse by verse until evening – so I say:

– Do you think about Éri?

The Old Voice reflects for a few seconds, the time it takes to adjust the Truth. The Truth blinks. Looks at the peonies. Says:

– Of Éri

112

I think

From time to time.

Éri's time had come and that's all there is to it.

In the dining room I still have the light falling on her smiling face.

Let's get back to the peonies. Looks at the peonies. One thinks their time has come. Death can also comes along *after* its time has come. How to explain time, a bit early or right on the dot? One has a time or another time, Ève's time, Éri's time. A century with two clocks. One shares everything, everything that is shared is completely different.

Ève Wisdom, totally different, to the point of bickering over it, Éri Wisdom

Their whole life their whole lives never said *we*

Maybe it's necessary to go back to the War of which their childhood was made, right away the brevity of the longevity made itself felt, the length of what is short, the blows of fate, the taste of soups, the derangedness of the reasonable father of the reasons of state. My mother's thoughts wind around the peonies. Conjecture about the beginnings of the story of Ève and Éri, one story composed of two stories. When we were little says Ève, during the war, maybe afterwards, in Germany we had big bowls of Quaker oats, *Quakers* we called them. I had one in 1917. Not Éri. They thought *I* was underfed, when it was her Éri who was suffering from malnourishment. Or in1919.

There is always a bowl, in the beginning in the genesis, one bowl, but two mouths, two sets of teeth with completely different destinies, a mockery of course and surprising, for no one will ever be able to demonstrate with any certainty what brought on the primal malnourishment scene. The only clue: the bowlful of Quakers has never been forgotten, not by Ève, who had the right and the other not, nor by Éri, who didn't have the right, though she was the hungry one, she who kept not only the most complete, the most perfect set of teeth of the whole family, but also, thanks to the strange magic of teeth whose brilliance resists time, a truly sustained air of youthfulness, and along with it, a mordancy, a cutting wit, a vivacity independent of the state of the rest of the person, so that Éri, unlike Ève, never had the disquieting doubleness of my mother in the nights without her teeth. The Quakers, says my mother, those folks who do good in America, sent over great cases of oatmeal for malnourished children. The doctor decided. I loved the porridge. It was a little on the sweet side. At school, during recess, Eric didn't have the right. In any case we each had a little box with a strap for our sandwiches. But there weren't any sandwiches, there was nothing in Germany in those days. So the mother, Rosi Klein, tells herself: the children bump up against each other inside me and no father? If things go on like this, how will we live? She consulted Dr Pelz, he tells her: two nations, two peoples, war on the horizon. When that war was over, right away starting with the Quaker porridge, they began making preparations for a next war. The best one can hope is that, the one getting the upper hand of the other in turn getting the upper hand, big and little sister survive the greatest number of wars possible. *Die Suppe*, says my mother, was delicious. *What's the problem?* cries my mother. Each time they talk about restaurants, Éri doesn't want Ève wants Éri doesn't want what Ève wants who doesn't see: *What's the problem?*

On December 1, 2006 I have a violent feeling of terror, once again; the gut twisters. The weather: stained-glass blue. Fear: mama didn't answer the phone. Interpretation 1: as usual. Books: Derrida. *Demeure, Athènes.* Photograph xvii. Ah! you say "We are owed to death"? Well, no, we refuse this debt! No. We refuse the authority of this anteriority, enough of this *Schuldigsein*, we can't accept this religion of mourning, etc. He says "we." You say "we" I tell him (I speak to him

114

through the stained blue glass, I telephone him over toward the sunrise) who, *we?* Who is we? You? On the left. On my right Proust vol. IV a notebook for the notebook of sketches for the dug-out sky blue notebook. *Once again the ungraspable:* The Sentence. Nominal. And elusive: chopped up, scattered about in its very utterance, prey to an internal violence and in advance struck by lightning, its own breath, wings, the future cut off. Like this: "*once again* [the twisters] *the ungraspable.*" Panting, it sits there, interrupted in its brutally aborted state, never published. It tears me apart. Its rending is of a miraculous freshness. A sentence without end boundless like God. At the conjunction of these two flashes of thought, a layer of light, substance of joy. The pane of stained blue glass sparkles as if the whole framed *View from My Study* had become a cathedral. *I have a vision of the next book*, pure life preserved pure.

Fear. Stage 2: but if the cause was not as usual she hasn't picked up the phone? Maybe she dropped the phone? Stage 3 right after: what if she – Are we not owed to death? No! No. No? Struggle. And him, Him, Derrida? No. We refuse this debt. You said *we*. My mother too. My mother neither. Isn't it December 2006? In the midst of battle. Fear 5. Fear 7. Because you think, a rational thought, a primitive thought, that Éri – preparing to depart – is there a law, are there examples – see Montaigne – that if one of them – as in the sketch of the sketch – a difficult text to decipher – "who lay [inert?] stone?] whereas the other not?" And what if it were the contrary? If the one led the other, "naturally." Éri leading Ève, the elder, led?

But if it were the opposite of the opposite? There is no battle. No nations rise up, not on one side nor on the other. It's you, that is to say me, who *once again* tortures heaven and earth. However, "[like those images called up by a music that seems unable to contain them]" now, in Manchester, I see one of them fold her belongings up into her big suitcase which to me looks inexorably padded, I see my aunt content to tell my mother: I've had enough, too tired now to sing her half of the immense song of a quarrel, I see my aunt still laughing when I tell her that according to Derrida "Manche sait se taire," my aunt who laughs no longer, sometimes it's my mother I see, dispossessed of her secret source of strength, deprived of her vital organs, stripped of her sister hence of mother father wars spouses archives, of Germanies nations victories of markets travels, heritages dictionaries all these strengths that as a pair we cling to, stripped of that calculable and incalculable sum that no notebook I could keep up to date will ever contain, and at the thought of this monstrous retreat that Time would inflict upon my mother, the *twist* – what if they pulled out my tongue? Turning sad thoughts over says Proust but *I* – I am the one who gets churned in the blades I have just noted that I've had a vision of a thick blue, and above all of a kind of crispness (I jot *crispness*, the sublime secret of arid summer, and the beauty of the word), Françoise calls me. Her cell phone, her words askew. She is outside Ève's door. Rings, rings, in vain. Cleaning day. Words barred. I put on shoes, coat. Keys! I run. Time, life, the street too long, too short. Downstairs a lady: aren't you Madame Cixous's daughter? Old lady. I call: Yes! over my shoulder. (Later: she knew me by the terror painted on my face.) I – elevator. Françoise – door. Ring, ring, ring. Hence. (During this entire eruption of pitch and ice only one lava: terror.) Keys. Three locks, three tortures. I go in *shouting:* mama! mama! (Cries: lava of terror, childish call for help, rage mixed.) (Vain hate: strident cries intended to send the enemy packing.) Silence. Dark bedroom. Dwelling place and cavernous sanctuary hollowed out of the rock, steams mingled with mists exuded by the rugs and the blankets, the cock, the train, no traffic penetrates the double-glazed windows re-doubled with the drapes brought from Algeria, the dogs, the neighbors, no real or telephonic animal disturbs the silence in the midst of which, from the visible and desperate appearances my anxiety throws up, my mother lies, and I cannot part the gloom in search of her with my trembling hands. Unnamable the fear of touching her and wreaking the supreme havoc. Mama! Mama! Light: ungraspable. Doesn't work. Dark bed in darkness. Cry. Silence. Light coming from the bathroom Françoise. Voice come from so far so very far, Athens perhaps: "What time is it?" Small. Asleep. Trying to find where she, who, time, place, in which year, Egypt, the tombs it was very interesting, coming back and finding in the midst of the confusion as last memory, the television show that bore her off toward two in the morning and returns her to me in mint condition, shielded from the screams of my phantasms by her ally the redoubtable the all-powerful Deafness. –I see my mother says that this is the latest I have ever wakened. – You didn't wake, I say. Even now you're not awake! I say. – It's the first time I've slept so late, says the astonished, antique Voice, she hasn't got over it, not yet. Her Voice, so far away, goes off again, drops off into the sinful state again. – I am sleeping, says the Voice, with a hint of animal stubbornness. – Come back, I say, curtly. Who knows what's keeping her there? I trust no one.

I have come back to my books. The stained-glass hour has passed. I remember: I had the Vision of the next book. It has left "the memory" of the sensation of joy, sensation of light sensation of crispness, all the sensations bereft of life, inert, peels, ghosts with names and no impetus. Everything has fallen *into the ungraspableness of the past.* Over there on the other side of the Allée Samuel Beckett the ungraspableness of the present mops the kitchen floor and runs Françoise at the wheel of the vacuum cleaner.

GET, GOTCHA

In October 2006 overexcited and gleeful my mother arrived, with her new hat and her suitcase, from Manchester where *she got 'em*. Everything evokes and adds to her sense of triumph. She got 'em. Her ninety-sixth year and the others. The verb *to get* she also got. This was some time ago, three, maybe four years ago. A bolt from the idiomatic blue. An expression strikes us. We thinks it's by chance. Makes its mark. Remains. It is, truth to tell, the very one we were waiting for. A button on a silk blouse, a four-centimeter-long safety pin, four o'clock: the hour of reckoning, an ordinary word of inestimable value, that takes us right to the sands that doze on the ocean floor, scolopendra, there's bell too, bells in the belfry, all the bells with their powers of resurrection from Strasbourg the city of her birth which is but a single bell, all these bits of matter, words and memories blended, which are for her the keys to the interpretation of the World. To get, is *everything*, that's all. Her jubilation, her crown, her Ferocity. The pride of the Fittest by dint of having as force only Art and as Art: that of living. Her flair for words whose ultra-strong magic looks like nothing. Flair, and not knowledge. To get *get* without any knowledge, presciently, via intimations she would be the first to decry, for she's "a realist." The idea that she may know what she doesn't know doesn't mean much. She is the proof. A proof of Literature. And without getting Get she's got it. It's like imagination. She has imagination. Ninety-six years old and off she goes to Manchester, prompted by her instinct to get *them*, all of them, the years, hers, Éri's only ninety-three, but also to get 'em and get 'em good, and all the more so as in Manchester a few folks are still extant with feats to their names, given their age, all over-nineties. All *candidates*. Experts, hence rivals. *She got 'em all.* The upshot of this inexpressible victory, no more accessible to thought than the why of a bell tower's charm, is youth, a radiance, which one suspects won't last much longer than the mildly splendid reflection on the dark, swollen underside of a storm cloud, but which is manifest. For the soul has the power, in extreme cases, to impress the color of a sentiment inside-out onto the external tissue. My overexcited mother is really not a day over ninety when she lands at Roissy. A phenomenon born at the confluence of the psychic system and dermatological chemistry. Flush. Elastic. Naturally this trophy, this appearance of youth, which is also a reality, is *projected* onto the screen by the ghost, totally ignored by my mother, but whom I recognize, of my mother Commander-in-Chief of the Algiers Maternity Clinic. Hence Manchester was the scene of a delivery. Maybe these were the *candidates* whom my mother's authority impressed with her faith in life, something she has in common with neonates. A faith, once God disappeared. To which let us add the phantom of the Queen Mother.

The hat is Éri. For her birthday. This one is going to outlast me she says. The old suitcase too. The suitcase is Ève. The hat and the suitcase won't forget the trip to Manchester. Every day one was elsewhere. When one gets to Manchester, things change. Every day one changes. Yesterday one had three invitations, tomorrow one has three invitations. Yesterday there was cousin Herbert ninety-years-old the only Jonas remaining on Earth. After one's coffee one visits a neighbor or vice versa the neighbor and the coffee. Over there people are on the dot. In the morning one ate salmon. Tomorrow is Kippur. Are we fasting? You, yes, but I'm the old lady who laughs. Fast, who fasts? I say I haven't time to fast. Time and tide, they're full of death and fury. By night tumors and paralysis by day typhoons – You are talking about death? asks my mother. You must have time on your hands. Pity. As far as I'm concerned it's too late. (1) I still have a thousand things to do. (2) I am not *in the least* worried. Fast? No. It's not time I'm short of, it's faith. Faith in whoever's in charge of That. All That – Faith – incredible isn't it? She laughs. Every now and then That comes back. I can't eat ham. All of a sudden. Faith is: That. It's something you didn't have that comes back. All of a sudden, the ham, says my mother – I can't. It's because of my father, who was so observant. For all the good it did him. He was killed on the spot. The captain wrote Omi that it was a shell. Next thing the leg was sawed off. A useless sacrifice. Still, God kept an eye on our parents. Their faith kept them from despair. Not from death. Death interests you? It's a thing you imagine. Your head is full of imaginary tornados and whales. Usually Sunday morning the various religions have their say on TV. Gone. A show every-one used to watch. All gone. The audience has no say in it. God. Gone. Without a word.

I hold out the phone. – For you, I say. Someone in Timbuktu. – From Timbuktu? Who is it? – I am Leonard in

Timbuktu. The male voice from Timbuktu: – I read the story about you in the newspaper *Libération*. I thought the article was extremely well done. I'm a photographer. – What article? – The male voice from Timbuktu runs on and on.

She looks me up and down. Disapproval: he wants to photograph my pimples this guy in Timbuktu!? – No. There's nothing to see. It's not worth your trouble. – He says he takes pictures. They're all talking about them in Timbuktu? You must have better ways to spend your time. That's the writer's *imagination* for you. She doubles up laughing. Don't come from Timbuktu for that. It's not worth it. – So I should turn in my plane ticket? – That strikes me as the sensible thing to do. Goodbye. She sits down. Another example of the power of the imagination. – Can you believe, everybody talking about my skin problems in Timbuktu. I forget his name. Leonard, I think. I should have told him: Stay in Timbuktu. I'll stay here with my pimples. Globalization, you see. You write the word Pimple and it turns into *der dicke Moby*.

At first I said: That's the Writer's Imagination for you. Then I said: That must be Pierre yourbrother, the African. – And your back? I say. I haven't put cream on her back since Manchester. You should show it to me. – I managed. I did the snake-lady. That Pierre, out to get me. At first I really thought it was a reporter, this Leonard. But *he didn't get me* after all.

Do you know why I'm saying that? You don't watch Television. All you're interested in is your Limbos. There's a commercial. In the centuries to come, all the archeologists who want to know what we were like will watch Television. I'd be surprised if they took much interest in your notebooks. I look at her. She still has the mysteries of Manchester on her back, That is something they won't see on Television. There's a guy says my mother, he has a competitor in another insurance company who did *better*. He thought he'd done better but he discovers that the other guy has done even better, I mean better than better. So he says to *us* behind his back: I'll get 'im! I wonder where this comes from. Maybe it's because he's number two. Not being the oldest, already as an infant in his stroller, he griped: I'll get 'im. Way back then, he was only a year old. Maybe it's hard to be the second. Like my sister and me. One does well. The other does something that's even better. She picked up this expression watching Television. I didn't know it she says, I thought it was a great expression. I told myself: one of these days, I'll get it. And bingo! I got it! Gotcha, I can say that about all kinds of things. About Éri too.

TO HAVE TO LOSE

She loses a letter. The letter was *there*. There. The Voice
gushes out. Somber psalm. *There.* I put the letter *there.* Swears
the black curdled Voice. On the little round table. The black
Voice lays it down. This morning, right there, waiting. The
Voice hardened, head lowered, horns jutting. She can still
see it. It's not *there* any more. There is not *there* any more.
This possibilized paralyzed paralyzing impossibility causes
my mother extraordinary pain. The Voice has the heavy
anguished furious sound of an unfairly tormented animal. It
tries to cope. Snuffles. Huffs. Suffers. Attests. Invisible gods,
speak. I put it there. She appears before us, pale head lowered,
eyes bulging. What has become of the letter? Evil, perfidious,
lugubrious forces are the answer to her question. What unbelievable spite, to attack the letter that was there. See to what
lengths a child, a son maybe or another, whoever it was, can
go, for one must be impelled by the most ancient animosities
to commit such prickly acts, acts that vex every inch of the
soul, harass the mind, keep one from sleeping, undermine

125

already weakened powers of resistance, that plaster the outer layer of skin and hence the psychic skin with allergic reactions, attack life's daylight. Gloom oozes from the little round table where the letter was, where it no longer is, sad radiation of an intolerable disappearance. I am not exaggerating. One mustn't, it goes without saying, judge the lost object, the quality of its life, by its weight or contents. Rather, one must take the measure of its importance by the trouble its loss occasions, the loss of the thing multiplied by the catastrophic effect of not knowing the conditions of its disappearance, a combination of factors that produces, who can deny, this hole in my mother's being. I take the measure of my responsibility: on the one hand, I cannot "reasonably" recount an event of Greek proportions. Hardly does my mother appear in the room where my brother and I are sitting, as per usual, my mother in the disheveled state of a character of an entirely other time, haunted, archaic that is, like something from the Bible or the Odyssey, than I have a strong sense of a rupture between two worlds, or two temporalities, accompanied by a serious problem of communication. For if in one world this event is protozoa-sized, in the other world into which my mother has tumbled overnight the event is a monster. So I wouldn't be fair to my mother's suffering if I didn't help this tale along with an appropriate sense of scale. Nonetheless I can feel it will be hard to demonstrate to my brother that a protozoa magnified not just by the lens of a so-called discredited unconscious but by the history of a long life whose lessons have made my mother someone ultra-sensitive to the too-real dangers concealed in the cracks, the drawers, the words, in the Great Swallowing Fish, a familiar and horrible figure in the memory of the Jonas family from which my mother on her mother's side, Omi my grandmother née Rosi Jonas, descends, no matter if this seems bizarre, is *really and truly* the gaping Monster since my mother is *in reality*, as we are her witnesses, in the state of a frail, trembling silhouette of an elderly woman tossed into the Maw. Perdition surrounds her. If she remembered the dream that woke her, even though, awake, her whole body still feels the grainy breath, that hurts her as if she had barbs in her arms, on her legs, even on her left cheek; and if remembering she dared to recount such silliness, one would rank this testimony with that of the Jobs or the Jonases. But she doesn't, more's the pity. To be half *Jonas* is enough, she prefers to think herself a *Klein*. Besides, the monsters, the Jonases, though nobody talks about them everyone steers clear of them. Steers clear of talking about them at least. For the Jonases are on the side of the Enlightenment and so are the Kleins. But, given time, here and there one sees dark formations dozing that can force their way in When The Time Comes. When The Time Comes has now set up shop in my mother's final chapter. Of course, the final chapter is wide open, in the culture to which we are attuned it can, I want it to, be as long as the whole volume, be subdivided, elevate itself and become a genre broader taller deeper than the century's old tale, it can turn itself into an epic and magic formula or be dry and testament, canoe or philosophy, but its name is *the last*. This being so, even if it takes me a few seconds to recognize my mother when she enters with a crown of bristling white locks, as if swept away internally by a gust of wind, I fairly rapidly make my way across my milder epoch toward her. And when my mother roars "who took my letter?" I get it. The letter that was there has become *The Letter from my Mother*. The key. The Verdict. Looking at her you'd think she'd lost half of her heart. One must be able to think that.

What she *sees* coming to her, coming against her, behind her back, sometimes looming thirty meters up over the balcony, sometimes gaping like a crack in the breakfast table when she opens an envelope addressed to her from the USA by a lady who, the missive says, is close to her whereas my mother knows no Rachel in the USA, nor in France, nor in Israel, nor in South America, makes her ill. Losing Éri is in the nature of things, commensurate, natural, she can accommodate the blow, lodge it within in the appropriate place. The Letter, this upheaval, this snatching, is like the plug of the world being pulled. It's too much. One doesn't know the enemy. It swamps her. In one fell swoop, unseen. This is due to the imagination. It's unimaginable. Who will explain? This pain absorbs my mother, all of her. I espouse her cause. My whales can wait. In a flash literature goes. It would be The Lost Letter all over again if, like my mother, I dishonored myself with a blind and unmerited condemnation. "Disappear" must be clarified. Literature withdraws, makes way for action, in this case "snatching my mother as quickly as I can from the Gaping Maw," she backs off, waiting, for under such circumstances I am everything to my mother. Let me repeat: I espouse her cause, that is my mother and what distresses her. In reality.

I look for the letter. She's right, it's no longer here. I look everywhere. I myself, without reaching my mother's paroxysm of despair, am baffled. This loss goes in search of a guilty party for my mother and finds: it's that madman who took the letter not yet stamped and threw it into the trash and beyond, so that not even the trash will cough up the prey. My mother's memory is a broken lighthouse. I don't for a second doubt there was a letter. I set aside the hypothesis of a guilty party (son or other), to which my mother desperately clings, for this seems to me unlikely, and dangerous: if the son threw out the letter, we'll stop looking. I look everywhere my mother herself, reasonably or absurdly, may have crazily "lost" the letter, for I am engaging in a principled search, an investigation without presumption. My mother ties a hanky to the foot of a chair. Every possibility is envisaged. In the fridge, under the cushions, under the bed, everywhere it cannot be. Room by room. Without emotion. Where others would throw up their hands, I go. The trembling, inflexible voice of my mother, in the kitchen, in the stairwell, the hunt gives her supernatural strength, blind, she orders me around as if she were at the helm of my eyes, my hands. I visited the cracks. I scour the world. Until nothing is left that hasn't been rolled over, turned up, except the bathroom. And that's where I find it. To my mother's joy. In a place where, having foreseen how the idiot would steal The Letter, she made it unfindable. My mother's life is as good as new.

The remarkable thing about losing this letter is that it happens again and again. She loses a letter. Every day: a lost letter day. Sometimes the letter has just come. Sometimes it is about to go off. My mother's siren wails. Every day is the first time. A thing like that. Monstrous. All is lost. It's not mother, it's other. I'll find it I say. I search and search: the letter is truly lost. We ask everyone, who took the letter? My mother's being is deeply wounded, on her face is painted the mask of an animal humiliated by human savagery, in her eyes wariness makes her gaze recede, slides it askance, one might see the glint of a dagger. The pain forever raw. I read: she has been betrayed. She is being mocked. Toyed with. Her needs ignored. Her innate sense of order flouted. She is not being helped to live, quite the opposite. Once the letter turns up and life is once again safe I attempt to share my suspicions with my mother: in my view somebody in her is losing the letters in place of her. An other. Perhaps she writes letters with the idea of losing them, that is letters to be lost. Thus she performs (that is she is acting, representing to perfection, to the point of fooling even herself) her own loss. She is a letter that might at any moment be snatched away and she wouldn't even notice. We could almost discuss staging this. Which does not preclude the purity of the anguish each time unique. I do not exclude the hypothesis that she loses the letter for me, before me, addressed in care of me: for each misplacement of the letter is a chance for me to rush to her rescue. It may be that this addressing is doubly motivated: to put my constancy, my competence, my trustworthiness to the test and at the same time cast me in the starring role, that of savior, either the principal or the only one of her powers of reason and her life. She loses, she is lost, she is saved. During this drama other foibles are satisfied: a predilection for resentment; a self-indulgent pleasure in confirming that she is surrounded by incompetents, the negligent, the absent-minded, the disorganized, which baffles her, she who is so completely the opposite. She wagers all her powers of suffering on a minor loss, a transference which has its advantages, even though these can in a trice turn against her. I could go on. Let me add that it is good to be aware of the tormented ground upon which our virtues proudly take their stand, without telling her, here I am quoting Freud, I am translating *lehrreich* by it is good to be aware, but this is better in German, it is rich in instruction, I want to persuade her that, though I am unable to calculate this, each time the letter is lost then found even if she has been horribly upset, she will nonetheless have reaped the benefits of a kind of relief good for heart and health. But she doesn't give a hoot about my commentaries. She wants her letter. That's all. Thinking about this I realize that I too want my letter, my literature letter. My mother of lost letters, my problem who gets out of bed later every day, the cause that turns me into a case of possession.

I try not to think about the future when the anguish of the Letter pilfered from my mother and her flesh will no longer exist, to be replaced by the anguish of no longer having to traverse my mother's tumultuous anxiety.

And lastly I discover, but at a later stage, that I take pleasure in the abyss brought about by the unlikely but stormy grandeur of the disaster.

Which brings me back to the whales.

The whale – where would I be, if my mother along with those she contains, beginning with my inner father, had not always had a cetacean magnificence. And to think she is unaware of this. In a twinkling she'd make *cétacée* (cetacean) rhyme with *c'est assez* (*that's enough*). On the one hand because she has a pronounced Germanic taste for doggerel, and the talent to match it. On the other because *Assez! – Enough!* is her favorite word. She thinks she hates excess. But she's the one who makes my pots boil. If I remembered the sublime text of 2004 that my friend J.D. lodged alongside the Whale, perhaps at its flank or even closer, in the secret entrails where narrators are all preserved from Literature, I could share the mystery with my mother here, but, hardly had he betaken himself to the scene after a struggle, triumphant in the end as usual but uncertain as ever to begin, against all the analytical psychological historical philosophical circumstances that wanted to throw him off scent, and which I had followed in the trancelike state into which such apocalypses throw me whenever my own blindness is at stake, than the light of indubitability faded. It was sublime, it was true. I remember I forgot, and J.D. preserved my memory. One has the keys and no armoire. So it is when events surpass us. So the tale of *The Life of Henri Brulard* is everywhere a fabric riddled with holes.

When I try to talk to my mother about the hereditary Leviathans she brushes them out of her thoughts like bees in her daughter's bonnet, she swats them back at me, she classes the rich monsters in what she calls "your leisure activities," and certainly the word *leisure*, the verb above all, has charms from which I make haste to profit. The idea that I take my leisure with whales suits me to a T. Since nobody else in the family wants them I'll take them, I tell myself. I might reproach myself this formidable license, an inheritance so

131

fabulous, it seems to me that in other families the inheritors would not have thought twice about accepting it. The moral soul of this colossal entity called family is mobile and jittery in all directions. Some think only of ridding themselves of an inheritance judged cumbersome or totally without significance too big, inedible, imaginary, a bad memory of war, of sea. What luck, for me. Or maybe what an obligation.

I could only with great difficulty have dragged this huge topic of conversation up alongside my mother, despite her recent conversion, above all televisual, to the animal question. "And the Whales?" I'll say one July day when I've harpooned her emerging from her shower on waves of Cyteal crowned with a few stray white locks spared by the incessant erosion that prints its mottled furrows over the surface of her body coining its dark medallions, leaving tooth-marked corollas on her whitening skin, pulling her toward me, whereas I would have loved to hug her, but it is increasingly dangerous to touch her; and in her scintillations, she gives off sparks, inventing beauties and graces that love is clearly capable of producing all the while thwarting with a flash the less positive aspects; all morning I'd been watching for her now my sun comes up at noon, one grows accustomed to this, one takes pleasure in these late yawns and stretches, all the other rhythms follow along since there is less time in each solar day I speed up, I cut my sentences short, my mother too, one lives as on a ship exposed to the buried reefs of continents, one speaks in a brief and powerful language, biblical in sum: Come! Here I am! Listen! Sit down! Here! One must be quick. (1) "your ears": Have you got your hearing aid – "your ears" – in? Nod: yes. (2) And the whales?: I venture out upon the heavy waters of the greatest dreams after many maneuvers and negotiations. She sits down – my dwarfling, my actress, my idol, my army – next to my desk and my mouth. Vigorously I push the powerful nominal phrase: "And the whales?" off in the direction of her ears. But the first shot misses. "The wells?" repeats Echo, Ève perplexed, innocent. Right away I throw a second line, which falls flat right away. "*Wahills*? What's that?" Alas, the closer one gets the further away one is. Fantasmagoria take over. My mother tries to picture this Wahill thing that escapes her, she searches her inner dictionaries. When I've shouted *Whales* a third time, in vain, and my mother goes hither thither giggling among the substitutes, ready if need be to push off toward far shores, Africas, Arctics, I fall back on my last resort. I had no wish to come to paper. Already so many heaps of paper between us, the entire skin of my mother can't repay my daily sins. Nonetheless we were at a standstill. I hesitated. There's always a first time to speak on paper. So we have come at last to the invisible circle that draws the fatal boundary of Ultima Thule. Once this line is crossed, no turning back. It would be another world, another life. I can already see colossal distances enter the narrow straits between my mother and me, the mutation that brings with it tele-technological revolutions in the forms of discourse, curves, timbres drying up. On the other hand my mother's handwriting is lovely, plump and shapely, baked to perfection, and I see myself already, wretched, collecting it. My mind wanders as Ève drifts this way and that astride this ghostly Wahill. So I hoist a banner of paper, asking: all right? It's nothing and it's awful. As if we were signing ourselves over to Mephistopheles, for me at least. My mother says: *Keine Wahl!* She laughs. She is in German. I imagine that in the hunt for the Wahill she must have turned toward German lands, perhaps consulted Éri, so that when the paper brings her back to me she settles for her mother tongue: *No choice.* It's all up. So this other time will have begun with the *Whale,* because of the Whale, as if summoned by the cetacean's occult power. There must be something in a Whale that I don't see, that I don't hear, and that defies us. Already the other time bears us away, already a powerful current carries us to the other side and we'll never return. I write this thing this word I throw damned sacred first last character the final Berechit has begun and in the beginning is a WORD in the middle of a vast sheet of white paper. Like this: *Whale.* My mother looks at it for a long time. She doesn't get it. It's unforgettable. Had I not made a note about this totally unexpected and crazy *end* to everything – end of time, endgame, end of the century – I'd have forgotten right away

This blank in time, in history, this event made of a blank-out, this time missing in the middle of time, my mother's silence at the Paper, my mother's blank face at Whale, my mother's stupefaction, whence mine, later on I am to compare them to the feeling of unforgettableness supposedly caused by *a* "performance" that knocks Stendhal-Brulard for a loop in 1800 when, at the start of his life as a madman in the world, he finds himself one day for the first time between the columns of a Napoleonic army, hedged on all sides by mounds of dead horses, but it's not that, it's the following day, in the evening, when, going out to a performance, it was Cimarosa's *Matrimonio Segreto* (he's crazy about it, about the marriage, about the secret, about Cimarosa, the performance, the army, Napoleon, the combination of massacre and music), that's when he sees it, the following thing, which is and isn't part of the show: the actress playing Caroline is missing a front tooth, and there you have all that will henceforth remain to him of divine happiness: the hole. Thus the imperial and military lavishness, the golds the blood the sabers the splendors of the suffering, this whole sublime catalogue recorded in *The Life of Henri Brulard* is to lead this incandescent soul to the sight of a gap in the actress's front teeth. I picture him in the second balcony of bliss spurring his soul onward with the help of the lorgnette, in advance utterly transported toward the land of chimeras which exists in reality a mere thirty meters away, leaning out right to his belt, almost overboard, already madly in love with the one whom he is getting ready to fall madly in love with, and suddenly like the lookout in the foremast, focusing his glass, pierced to the heart by this unexpected trait, that makes the object of his desire one of a kind, unique. Truly, what could be more dazzling than this absence of presence, what could be more exciting than the apocalypse of a tooth whose absence is precisely centered, like the center of the world where the Babylonian Chastisement is in full swing. And the soul at hearing a great voice cry: She has fallen, she has fallen, The Great One, the woman in scarlet and purple, she who told herself just before she fell: I reign as queen, I am not a widow and never will I mourn. And that's all that remains of the secret marriage of the lover of life with the land of the Apocalypse.

And when my mother stares at the Paper, there is a blank unforgettable as the non-tooth in the mouth of the Celestial Voice, of which I immediately take note. Nothing so forgettable, as the narrator that Proust makes his prophet tells himself, nothing so forgettable as the unforgettable sound of the spoon, for if one lets the wave pass, if one doesn't right away yoke oneself to the trace, if one doesn't throw oneself heart and soul after the invisible animal, abandoning all other business, if one lets oneself be turned from the essential by society, despite all the recommendations, forever vain, of the prophet within me who foretells the whale within me, the event without a name vanishes, slipping away as powerfully as a dream and all the more imperceptibly as it seems insignificant. Three words: Ève white whale. Underneath, the date. Silence is always much bigger. Neither all the singer's teeth nor all the sweetness of her song can match for greatness the immortal power of the missing tooth, that is the more than tooth.

I was flabbergasted, at the sight of my flabbergasted mother, her gaping Seventh Seal Lamb's head.

135

What's happening? I ask myself. We'll never know. Silence fills the Study, for about a half an hour, says the sensation. *About*. The moment when the silence comes to an end is mysterious too. Finally my mother lifts toward my eyes all the world's uncertainty: "Is that German?" Regretful. This word is German, and she doesn't recognize it, at last she breaks the seal and she doesn't enter. A line of bad thoughts stops her. She feels herself in the position of "candidate" whose status she has so often evoked. Only now it is she who stands before the undecipherable inscription. I myself can't come up with the word she seeks, I don't know from what city to call to her. I no longer remember how, suddenly, we are yanked from the brink of the quid pro quo. I didn't write that down. One loses the second that precedes the salvation. Now, thus after, my mother gives a howl of laughter. Saved, what's more she's so happy she no longer has the least desire to stop, she reads and rereads *Whale* yelping from one laugh to the next as if, to get across the void, she were leaping from rock to rock. The frozen lake behind her. It was nothing but a Whale! Now life that was caught in the grip of a sad enchantment, stunned voiceless and faceless, returns with great walloping laughs, whinnies, canters, tosses its mane of freedom this way and that. – Wa-hale! What on earth do you want me to do with that? I'd have to go a very long way to see one. I don't get it: are they fish? Awful to be so huge. (All this warbled to the tune of Cimarosa.) Such a big fish in the sea. So big and so nice, and for what? – But I say God created the big cetaceans on the fourth day right in the beginning and before all the human animals. – Whales first? Stuff and nonsense. He made a mistake. He wanted to create man, he created a whale: *And that's not it*. My mother re-creates. God goofed. A Whale: a man manqué. Between the two of them, therefore, will always be the ghost of memory that makes the two former halves of the androgyne tremble. – We don't know them, says my

136

mother. At that moment, having quickly scanned her memory right back to the beginning of the beginning, she hides within herself a little bright-eyed brown-haired girl pedalling her bicycle round and around Strasbourg Cathedral. – I don't remember whom it was it swallowed. Not Abraham, or Isaac? I say: Jonas. – Ah! I should have known. How could my mother "forget" Jonas, i.e. herself and every single bit of her mother? Aren't you a Jonas? – I never thought that was the belly we came out of. My uncles couldn't even swim. Nor could my mother and aunts. One is born Jonas one is in the cavern. One knows the fish, says my mother, but suddenly one sees something like That something one never sees except when one finds them high and dry. I saw the word on the piece of paper without any trouble, but I couldn't put a name to this word. I think I beat around the bushes a bit, and then I'll come up with it, says my mother, I waved away the wa-hole. I am afloat in the Universe. Because I'm a Jonas? Maybe the Jonas family in her has fled totally, it is organized for flight. Unless it's the opposite; it's the Kleins who throw the Jonases overboard.

It is, in fact, incredible and magnificent that she should have forgotten, "forgotten" that is her own mother's name, and even the letters and archives of her maternal name, passed on to me in its original state of having been swallowed up as if it was for my sake she forgot, bequeathing without bequeathing, by forgettation, so much for the monster and all it contains. Even the fact that the secret name of my father Georges her husband the Jewish name of my father for the Book of Books turns out to be Jonas too, she has totally forgotten this by an act that has been transmitted to the whole family, all by itself, as at the opening of the Seventh Seal silence falls, so that I am left by myself, with this Jonas cast up like the shell of the Seventh Seal cast up by the angel on the edge of the Book – until

– I once saw elephants what they eat aren't tidbits. (Now

my mother moves back from the brink toward dry land.) But the camel is the best. The camel is my mother's touchstone. Hats off, says my mother, it can go for days without eating or drinking. It is going to disappear. Who needs camels? We've got cars. It's like the "It-Remains-to-Earth" restaurant. Such a charming place she always wanted to eat at one day. All gone! She is disconsolate. She proclaims the news to passersby. The period of mourning lasts for a week. No more It-Remains-to-Earth! A shame! Nothing lasts and everything disappears. At each disappearance disappearances besiege her. How long can one outlast the It-Remains-to-Earths the all-you-can-eat-for-next-to-nothings. The old Renault is still going strong. Whale in German? Gone. Let me think. It's not a word I have much use for. The names of the uncles who have disappeared: disappeared. Don't know any more what the Whale is called. Here, I can tell by the gleam in the middle of her eye, she misses Éri. Either Éri would remember and this would relieve my mother of the task, or Éri too would have forgotten, which would boost my mother's morale. Guess what happened to me today? A hole. A wa-hole in stead of a word. It doesn't matter. When I don't know one I find another! She laughs. She imagines what other word might fill the wa-hole. Guess what happened to me yesterday: my trousers. I put them on backwards. I noticed the elastic was in front. But since I'd already put on my shoes, I didn't change. It could be worse. I lost something I hadn't lost. The blade for my parsley chopper. I searched every single drawer with a flashlight. I gazed at my chopper with great yearning. And hey presto! The blade! right inside. You've no idea how busy an old lady's life can be. They don't lose things. One thing they lose is their heads. And the rest follows suit.

"Éri," my mother sighs. She stares vaguely off at the ghostly silvery smiling image, Éri who doesn't speak, since when, months have passed, Éri whose reflection I perceive in my mother's ever-so-slightly lunar drift. "Éri." Now these syllables alight, fluttering, on a hole. Éri is full of holes. The sounds of Éri come a little astonished out of my mother's mouth. Éri is no longer hailed. My mother hauls her up, a huge, imponderable shadow from a planet that has left the solar system

Éri,

says my mother, and the sentence doesn't come. I listen.

A moment later – it has therefore made its invisible way through long invisible waters – my mother's voice speaks up and says to me: "When I have things to tell her, obviously, I can't tell her anything." The sentence's music is a fabric woven of practical, objective, monotonous observation, heightened, trimmed with tense irritation which stands for and replays the thread of irritation that tied Ève to Éri throughout the checkered reverie of a ninety-three-year voyage. So nothing has changed. Still there, the Erieve affect, that aura of authority and rebellion, that faithful little mutiny. As usual, if my mother heads one way, my aunt goes the other. So Éri is still here, the same as ever, ready at the drop of a hat to say no or yes or vice versa. She tugs. They tug. My mother has things to tell her. How do you say Whale in German? Éri the guardian of German. My mother of French. In English they are neck and neck. "But the last time we talked on the phone, she was already saying *I've had enough*" says my mother. She agrees with this. For the first time Éri resumes her vivacious airy indefatigable spirit of resistance to Ève (who gives her life the ravishing allure of some kind of pig-headed Albertine, bound-fugitive, surreptitiously disobedient always dressed with exquisite taste for she was her own Fortuny) in a phrase so apparently simple and familiar. She said: *J'en ai marre, I've had enough*. What could be more totally indefinite, hence infinite, than this rejection of what one has had, as if my aunt had poured the world into a hole of sea.

Now these words – *j'en ai marre* – last flourish of my aunt, who picked up her French in Paris when, in answer to the call of my mother the commander of their destinies, she joins her there, Éri the most elegant little silhouette in the anxious, greenish flux of refugees who disembark on Lethe's quay, Gare du Nord, Paris in 1931, she becomes an apprentice in the great Fortuny couture workshop only, unfortunately, in the fur department which is very hard and doesn't interest her, there are lots of Russians as well, it's not the same immigration wave, they have come because of communism, in Germany they didn't care much for the Russian immigrants, they were beggars. Poles. And that's where nonetheless she very quickly picks up French, her own French, a unique brand, magnificent, shimmering, voluble, whose fabric embroidered with birds of paradise, neologisms, ellipses, with grafts and audacious appliqués of German and English words she deploys for me, making my aunt the creator of an inimitable, rapid, rich, sporty, incorrect language that my mother was never, their whole life long, to stop correcting though in my view everything is pearls and jewelry and each time my mother pares away, polishes, I for my part egg on and cultivate the éridiom – but furtively, discreetly, for no way I could take Éri's side and not Ève's –

Now here we have the words of the last phone conversation, my aunt, or Éri, or the young-girl-in-bloom, forever-desirous, who outdid herself laughing right up to the Manchester days, and that she has kept on hand for just such an occasion, elected, threaded with her needle in French, on her way out the door, in the language that is neither more nor less hers than any of her languages, but is the one in which she finds possibilities her sense of fantasy appreciates, the casualness, the way they fall – my mother not only receives them but does not even correct them, on the contrary, something warns her, she clings to them, she salutes them, she repeats them, vaguely understanding that they have a je-ne-sais-quoi chic. Underneath the Parisian tulle. That Éri chose them especially. Fashioned with mathematical force. Less for more. No grandiloquence. We owe no cock to Asclepius, says Éri. And Ève, though it gave her pause – just for a second – nearly said: no, the sun is not yet down – had the good sense to say yes, to Éri. Yes. In any case *there's no point in letting things drag on.*

Words Éri spoke only once. And Ève never. Except to repeat them on Éri's behalf. Ninety years at least stitched unstitched together, at the end now Éri now Ève, now the two of them forget their ear, one hears them then, the two Deafnesses jabbering away, a conversation other, voices lifted in totally disjointed and extravagant speeches, which never prevented, even if in my view they drift toward opposite banks, a bizarre fidelity keeping them in unfathomable proximity, as if, when voices lose sight of each other irreparably, the voice of the blood keeps them clear of the abyss. Perhaps they are a two-sistered single being, I tell myself. I watch my mother's eyes send Eri things to say, she knows not where. One can't imagine in what shapeless bottomless gulfs the soul lets itself down in no time in order to go and consult some oracle that doesn't pick up the phone. But sitting on the shores of my mother, my body of water, I see time pass. Her mind wanders in the depths. She can't help it. These things are out of control, these expeditions without a compass. Then – as if, lifting the corner of a black oilcloth sea, one could make out – so far away it seems one approaches the limits of the visible, a form, incredible, that one believes one really recognizes a hump appears, and as if these vast sheets of water had been, to my mother's flying eyes, the vast swaddling clothes of the memory cut and stitched by Éri, as if, while I'd left her alone in her armchair, in the middle of the cane-less, sister-less world, one was nonetheless forced to notice that some phenomena are inexplicable, for example that my mother felt she had seen Éri's familiar silhouette. I think it, but I won't say it, she tells herself. Whereupon, as froth sprays everything, out comes the Whale in German. – *Ein Wahlfisch!* It seems like a foreign word to me! says my mother. It makes no sense to think Éri prompted me, thinks my mother, some things one mustn't think, but I think that thinking, it's not as if one had any choice. *Ich habe nicht die Wahl.*

THE BLUE NOTEBOOK

The Blue Notebook episode has been waiting since the dawn of this book. I have been preparing the materials for two years. I know this from the dates on my different notes. It's as if it were already written, though it isn't, not yet and forever not yet. So here it is. Right here. More than once I might have thought: (1) That I was going to write it immediately, that is tomorrow, witness five Post-its where it says: tomorrow: The Blue Notebook. Or: Tomorrow finish page 5a. Then: The Blue Notebook. It's a hodgepodge. It comes back again and again. It comes and goes. (2) That in the end, the book gathering speed, careering toward its end, caught up, fleeing and fleeing me, The Blue Notebook moment escapes, has passed maybe it would be best to abandon the theme. (3) Maybe these slips and slides, these delays are signs. Certainly they are they demand an explanation. I could look for them later in another book. For, another sure thing, The Blue Notebook strongly exists, with an idea and a shadow, but also the pale folder where materials have collected. And there is also The Blue Notebook itself. The Blue Notebook is not a fiction. And yet, in my opinion, it is The Fiction itself, it is perhaps, I tell myself here, this strange powerful, apparently invisible nature that exerts such a force of repulsion – it's not repulsion, on the contrary, but a magnetic force, both irresistible and impossible to improve on, each time I start or turn or get ready to approach it, as if The Blue Notebook had a soul and that soul a desire, something comes along to distract me, a last-minute emergency, a fork in the story, the unexpected arrival of a character or some suffering that must be received first, and all these incidents that temporarily cause The Blue Notebook Chapter to be set aside seem dictated by the subject itself, as if by its inner motions. After which everything takes place naturally in a kind of twilight, I see nothing, I don't think of it. I don't completely forget about it, for on the sorts of outlines whose ladders help me descend into then ascend again from the mine of each day's writing, each time I see the title "The Blue Notebook" flashing, but each time at a different level. In the end chance alone will decide I tell myself, that is, the book. I don't decide: I won't write The Blue Notebook. This would be presumptuous on two counts. The Blue Notebook is already written and only God knows if and how it will get past the fine spiderwebs of my resistance. I should write: Godalone – for this is a special version of God between God called Godalone, who is, for such is how he appears to me, hence in dream, the God who dwells in books. Thus I met him in a fairly thick volume, an anthology of God, in which each chapter, arranged like a song from Hell, was called God. There were fifty or so of them: God, God, God, etc. Each of them unique, the one and only, God I, God II, etc. All this is connected to The Blue Notebook. Also, I should call my resistance Spider. It, or she, is in fact the maternal author of an infinite number of webs (analogous I tell myself to the chapters of God) miraculously

144

perceptible only when, for a fraction of second, I glimpse the admirable work of this shield of silvery threads of saliva shining in between me and the world, which happens only when, with a twitch of my hand, the marvelous web suddenly comes undone, rolls up, vanishes, to be replaced on the spot by another, different, and also bewitchingly splendid one. I've also taken note of the state of expropriation into which I am thrown by my brief stabs at starting to write at least the introduction to the episode. Three lines later it's no longer my hand, no longer my writing, what rushes along with supernatural speed is the hand of hallucination, the handwriting that looks galloped away at the orders of a being – whom my mother might call the infamous demon who sits astride my shoulders – and vanishes in the middle of the page, because I can't keep up. Moving faster than itself, it often trips up and commits many slips of the tongue, giving it a sloppy, nervous, arrhythmic look. In it moreover I recognize a respiration, a musculature, a strength that frightens me a little, an invincible obstinacy, this is what stops me, this feeling that in The Blue Notebook, whatever may come to pass on this earth, there's something, a spirit, that's absolutely invincible. As if The Blue Notebook were thinking: run away all you like, in the end I'll win.

The Blue Notebook is not mine. This too can be refuted. I admit my manner of affirming this non-possession is equivocal. Am I not persecuted and therefore possessed by The Blue Notebook? I don't want to know about it, that's all I can say. It awaits me. This I know. My mother keeps it. I have happened into her room at midday and seen her sitting, completely absorbed in keeping it, and I promptly withdraw. We have traveled with The Notebook. It and my mother are never apart. Of her splendid strength, now faded, once lodged in The Backpack, her suitcase, her armor, her coat of arms, this object which has acquired a prodigious added value in the life and history of my mother, as she daily recalls, she's The Backpack, she's the one who invented it in the 1930s, The Backpack is the avant-garde, by means of The Backpack all the way to eternity via wars and the Desert, all that's left is The Blue Notebook. Once upon a time The Backpack held papers, food, water bottle, books, checkbook, handbag, keys, change purse, the world and The Blue Notebook. Once upon a time ended in 2005. By an unforeseen turn of events, now it is The Blue Notebook that is in charge of keeping The Backpack going. Because she can neither part from The Notebook, nor carry it in her hand or in a shoulder bag she finds herself unable to give up The Backpack. There is no other solution. Her weakened frame can no longer support weight. However one must carry The Notebook. The Notebook cannot be trusted to anything or anyone. So you see the problem. The idea of making a second notebook has never crossed her mind. Thus, paradoxically, The Blue Notebook keeps The Backpack alive and yet how much death The Notebook contains. Each time she tells me: I must show you my notebook, I say yes. She waits for me with her notebook and I don't go. I go and I break my promise. Did you see my flowers? says my mother. An old woman in bloom. I take my time in front of her flowers. Six little planters full of dwarf pink geraniums. I look at my mother's flowers. It is a ritual. I look at my mother looking at me looking. Little old pink geraniums. Holding on. All of a sudden the time is up. Quick, I leave. – The next time, my mother says, I'm going to show you my blue notebook. Yes I say. The next time. Little by little it becomes harder to put off next time until next time. Not that my mother's patience wears thin. She waits, pure little old pink perennial. But the next time, hiding in the pink geraniums, she tightens the screws, murmuring that I'm going to be caught out in the end with my manner of saying yes and doing no. It becomes harder and harder for me to think about the ineluctable encounter with The Blue Notebook, I have so delayed, deceived, denied, effaced, all the detours, the missed appointments make a mound inside me, whose volume increases week by week, it would be remorse except that it has a real shape, vague because of the distance but accusing, disquieting, a tumulus of broken promises, one could say, in whose vicinity pink geranium plants come into bloom with a distressing constancy.

The objective impossibility began after my mother's bout with pneumonia. Still swaying and drunk from the voyage, unsure even of being back on Earth, in that in-between state into which one drifts after having been cut off from reality by a brutal sojourn in illness, we had been to all the banks, they seemed to be everywhere, I dogged along behind my mother as usual into this kind of den, but it was a gloomy journey, mama wandered, staggered, from chair to chair we went, it was a matter, it seems to me, of powers of attorney, at the counter we requested powers of attorney for one another, the word power of attorney, this mingling of mama and me, I counted on my mother for the life that I was trying to haul back up toward us from the depths of pneumonia, wrecks, I can scarcely see us, haggard we go to the Credit Lyonnais to the Credit Commercial I watch us from I don't know what year to come I watch us drift from rock to errant rock with their prophetic consonantal names CL is you, is us, I was sick to find myself so adrift before the counter of time adrift with my mother at the helm, a ghost ship thick bilious towering black waves, in the end I no longer know where, Rue du Petit-Promontoire perhaps, there was the Caisse d'Épargne way up at the end of the road, the Cocyte one might have said, and there, I gave up, we'll go later I say, this is crazy, we are going to lose our lives for our savings, exhaust my mother in such sinister, inhospitable places, to come out of the Hospital and enter the Bank, even if the Siren is attired in mama's heart-rending garb – as if one gave death leverage, my strength failed me, I no longer know which of us brought us back to which bank, who heading off again dragged along with her the final images of this last voyage. I need to show you The Blue Notebook, my mother said. That was January 2005, the Hospital Bank Credit Proxy boxcars of death. We got off at Geraniums Station. My mother on the phone with her sister: Hélène put her foot down. Or put it off until tomorrow. The so small voice totters. Don't do that to me! I say to the Voice. Get back up here!

As a City surrenders to a City, an army to an army, a feeling of terror to a phone call from God, on January 27, 2007 I bowed to fate. Why this day, this hour, because it was impossible. Things couldn't go on this way. I switched to another brand of cowardice.

We are having dinner. In a thousand and one details she tells me about her trip to Lisbon with Éri, twenty years ago. She relives the trip, I cut it short. We should have gone ten years later she says because after the Olympics there's the bridge, much better, off she goes to Lisbon all over again via the new bridge. One was searching for somewhere to eat the local codfish fritters, Éri didn't want to, they didn't find any. They took the bus to Fatima she's a saint there were a few pretty little villages. Next Fatima was a church. There were only two other people, two Jews. Four Jews? I say. Two says my mother. Nothing for us to do there, with that Fatima. Éri thinks her blue cloak is pretty. I take her home. She is tottering. The road to Fatima leads to The Notebook. I look at the Allée Samuel Beckett without Éri. We cross. You are no longer here. I can no longer beat around The Notebook bush. In the garden she tells me: the life insurance. Frugal with her sentences. The grass is green and flowery. We walk by it. In front of the door I ask: why? – It's for the estate taxes. I forget. There's enough there. She thinks about the burial. I am buried alive. One looks at the pink geraniums. I kiss her. She is small. I look at her size in the mirror in which we will be mirrored smiling and hugging. Some are wilted, she doesn't notice. Thanks to the amaryllis. There's still one flower coming up, says my mother, it's quite decorative. The details of the apartment bear witness to the thorns in my heart. I leave to Balzac the thirty pages of lavish clichés, the overabundance that makes the ugly beautiful, the necessary unflagging ecstatic exactitude required to describe my mother's cluttered interior. The Blue Notebook awaits us. Aha! cries my mother.

The Notebook can wait. There's a prologue. Here we are seated on the chairs in front of the impossible metal desk I've never been able to get rid of for somebody inside my mother finds it still serviceable. – I went to the Bank, says my mother. Next I went for my ears. There I went to the toilet. Naturally I wonder where in this labyrinth of goings she wishes to lead me. Ah! I forgot says my mother, ingenuous preteritive, I mean I remembered but I didn't dare tell you: I went to get an estimate for the funeral. – Let's discuss that another day, I say.

A big hard-covered notebook, strong as an ox, with a small white label "2007" and perforated pages.

Mama lays it out flat. Holy book. Middle of the first page: *Contents* underlined. 47 pages. 47 sections, says the page, reads my mother. The handwriting clear, strong, beautiful, spidery, noble, modern, mama. It is Friday. A fine day, cold. We are at the little round table. The whole scene takes place in my head in the painful future-present. My mother in the middle is burning. Mama. Her wiry white hair, her serious little face, led by her large nose bent over the notebook's pages, reads each page with care blue bible of accounts. She reads aloud, slowly clearly. Her face comes away from her face, a body follows, and my mother sits down in another scene, which I have alreadylived, both scenes turn around the Book, but it's the same scene, with the poignant difference of a today, I've never experienced this before I tell myself, I'm transported, but the joy of the event is all but unbearably sad. I in the grip of the Times that will only come again as ghosts of themselves. Terrible humble times messengers of suffering. Such a small eternity, I wish I were only at mama's, looking with the helpless anger of the least of the dragons, at my mother's account book, but this is not at all what's happening. Never in nightmares have I been so ill with being, I'm the merest mental debris, I'm despondent, I wish I could jump on a plane, find spring, run down the street with my beloved a long time ago, but there is no airplane to return from time, and no train either. We are in real life. Reality is a small room two nightmares hold in a vise. It's not my fault, it's my mother and her book that haunt me so. She herself is observing the rites of a ceremony whose returns I already see and dread. I recognize the officiant and the affect that sets me afire: I've alreadyseen my mother, led by her nose which age lengthens toward the pages of a book of spells, stirring up the characters of The Book in her broken voice, beaten down by the pretensions of age, threadlike. I saw myself listening to a battle between my mother's vitality and nature's abstract machination. The battle occurred on December 25, 2006, between Hanukkah, that is, my mother and the lights, on the one hand, and on the other the Law, monstrously crazy in my view, that avariciously cycles life. We light the first candles. This scene is a landmine. All by itself it's a scene that hides another scene. Let's say that the hiding is reciprocal. When my mother celebrates Hanukkah, she feasts and feigns at the same time, honestly with subtlety, for my mother doesn't believe, but she finds a charm in the belief she does not have, what remains of religion is the *ambiance* she says, she is glad to hold on to the ambiance, to the word as well, especially the word, the words. It's the same for Hanukkah, the charm, the words, the lights, the story, every year she forgets it, therefore I can tell her again, she never throws out a thing that might make life more agreeable the envelopes, the containers, the jars, the lids, the skin, the body. Last December 25, a day of bottomless sorrow I was thinking, everyone leaves, my good friends, the woman, the man, Éri, life emptying itself out life empty, I ask mama: have you never lost the courage to live? Knowing that she has never lost anything if I ask the question it's because I am curious about *the form* the answer will take. And the response snaps back, naked, clear, tranquil as mama's soul: Never. She's reading The Blue Notebook. She's reading *The Book of Common Prayer*. Deciphers the first page. Same concentration. Devotion, the same. It's a matter of giving life to the book. The Voice comes from the bottom of time: studious. Lesson. The language is the same: in both cases it is Hebrew. The difference is the book. The Blue Notebook clean large practical, one can add pages. *The Book of Common Prayer* looks like a dust mote. Mama. Pretty gentle disciplined head. Her pink sweater. So thin. Thinner and thinner. I track the dwindling. How far how long. When her voice quavers a column of figures firms it up. She communicates to me injects transfuses transmits what is called: Contents. The word Contents. These begin by "In case of Death." My mother pronounces in case of death. The word death imparts a little phonic satisfaction. I don't watch, I don't listen. Mama reads. She stops. Here a figure is missing. She completes a line her finger underlines: lot number 5. She writes with application. Like she prays. The secret is in the application. Slowly I slip into an anesthetic drowse. The candles go down slowly too. A yelp: where's my will? I hear from under the anesthesia. We can't be there. Ha! Here it is. The page of the notebook is folded over and taped to the inside cover of The Blue Notebook. Mama wets her finger, unfolds. Mywill.

The grimoire must be divided into two equal parts. But my mother is having difficulty adjusting Gri to Moire. She tries different combinations. Grim and Oire? What do you think? One might also imagine Groi and Mire. Should I buy Pierre a share of the Strasbourg property? We discuss at length. This is beyond me. I say we might divide the body among the children. Ève approves. Vaguely I wake. Frozen. The square meter. Gri says my mother doesn't mean anything. We must come up with a better rhyme. Mama moves on. In mama's glasses the candles glow. We notice the equality then the inequality of the candles. I limp, she races on ahead. Translate I say. She translates all these Hebrews into a language in which German and English words are juxtaposed and deducible. The figures: in French. Frozen. Between 5,000 and 7,000. – Stop, I say. – Never, says my mother. Now, the ones in the middle get lowered one after another. "The extremists are still resisting." Says Ève. Finally the extremist on the right falling asleep the extremist on the left fires off a last volley. It's Ève, I tell myself. She's thinking: extinction. She says: That Hitler, what could he have been thinking? I don't get it. A group of people that speaks all the languages. She doesn't get it. Me neither. Ève is so un-"Jewish," in other words, so deeply "Jewish," so elsewhere, so otherwise, so singular, so fictional, at the same time so outside time. She is not like anyone else. Less and less. She stands up. She grows bigger and bigger and radiant. She shuts The Blue Notebook. "From tip to toe" she says. As if she were arming herself for her chivalry of a life. This scene goes along with thoughts of the coming year. Thecomingyear dims its festivals' feeble lights. – I have some *Kartoffel Puffer*. Traditionally German potato fritters have consolatory virtues. – *Pfannkuchen* I say. – *Puffer*, she says. I eat some: Ève's holy wafers. Holes bored under my thoughts. The flame in the apartment. Éri smiles from the wall. Everything nice and tidy. The Order of the

Bric-à-Brac. Museum. Who will do the inventory? Little face, so small, I look for a spot on which to plant a kiss.

To wrap it all up, she shows me the pink geraniums. What a shame the amaryllis is finished. I let myself be led around. A halt in front of each plant. From one plant to the next. And it's a trap: Oh! cries my mother. I went to see about the funeral. She's worried about this funeral. I went to get an estimate. You will organize a lavish funeral. I want first-class bargain basement. We aren't going to have an argument over this thinks my mother, all set to argue. It's like for the fish. Do you think it has to be expensive? Why? It's the same codfish as from the market. No fancy fish! She makes a stand for her camp, her field, her plot of ground. But I don't rise to the bait. – I hate those big padded boxes she warns. What to call my mother's courage? This intrepidity, the firmness of the mind that looks dying in the eye, this is not the time to throw a tantrum, one must neither rush in nor delay, nor cut the cord as long as the blood is still flowing. Precision and fidelity to the pulse beat. Same thing for the estimate. No padding under any circumstances. I saw it's very expensive. 31,000. How can this be? It used to be 20,000. To my way of thinking that's a lot of money. What do you think? asks my mother. She thinks that I'm thinking, I tell myself. And already later she means to blame me for not having given her the advice she could have ignored. My face falls. I haven't the strength to say to mama: I haven't the strength . . . it's too close. Your funeral will be the death of me. It's as if we were helping it along. We should have looked after this before, says my mother. In my nightmare I fall to pieces, I'm at the end of my tether, the others do their work and are radiant, I am in ashes, I can hardly take myself away, I want to go home I ask everybody where my return ticket is, but as in The Blue Notebook, they tell me there's no such thing, it's a one-way. I'm terrified, I plead. I'm reassured to see my mother come up joyfully and welcome me. So, though devoid of body my shadow is still recognizable. She asks me whether I've been. Her pressing, luminous, normal tone drags me back from the funeral I was getting lost in. To the Museum. I haven't been to the new Museum, but my mother has. Hence there's a scene "My mother inaugurates the Museum." – Never again to that Museum, it had no interest whatsoever. We had lunch in the Cafeteria I ordered fish, couldn't even tell what kind of fish it was. My cousin had a different fish. For dessert I had a disaster. They called it a tart. In reality it was apple baked on some inedible stuff. After that we wanted coffee and it wasn't possible. And the chairs, dreadful. And the exhibition: boring. You shouldn't have let me go. Those heads of State. The king of the chickens who wants to round off the tale of his reign. Each time quick he lays a museum. Then, quick, death does its work. *Und jedes legt noch schnell ein Ei. Dann kann der Tod dabei.* Her mythology makes her roar with laughter. Quick, each of them lays one last egg. Next, quick, death does its work. She cries laughing at her translation of Wilhelm Busch. The little pink geraniums sum up the extraordinary sobriety of my mother's grandeur. I gaze at them with the mystical mystified limited emotion as befits this economy for me totally inimitable. The row of little clay planters is unaccompanied by any train of sensations of light and happiness that would have inundated summer mornings spent in a house for instance in Algiers. The little pink flowers, one-third of whose petals are withered, do not summon to their aging heads any toasty sensations dragging along with them a train of marvels preserved in amber, no cobblestones. I add. I open. I multiply geranium by its rich etymological hoard, I convoke the crane that conceals its name *geranos* in the meager bouquet, the screechy bird ger! ger! as if the flower in its tenacious structure were the flower of old age, I graft a gerontology, I nestle into the foliage of phantasms. My mother, no. No ornaments.

154

The price of things is the things themselves. So I tell myself, one can therefore live in the moment, do without Venice and immerse onself in Life. Ève is able to do the little geraniums, without reading without lyre. No hope I tell myself of some last word, some final truth from her, sad sort of being that I am perpetually hobbled by the need to scribble notes, I passionately admire the model, but I will never be able myself to sustain the spirit of naked geraniums. Already the geraniums were totally mama.

She clucks she laughs: we've played a darn good trick on fate, haven't we once again both of us ninety-seven and counting? And still so much to be fixed. The timer for the garden is on the wrong side, it needs to be moved. I go off again. I turn around I gather mama into my eyes, let me keep her shining eyes, I can cross the darkness of the world, I cover the ground twice as fast as when I am with mama. My legs walk. I am living to the end. I precede. I die before me. Behind me the little pink geraniums

ÉRI GOES ON AHEAD

For once Éri leads, my mother trails behind. But one might think the contrary. This causes a moment of confusion on December 15, 2006. Here's how. My mother's cheerful voice telephones me: *Éri, wie geht's?* Never before has my mother called me Éri. Am I Éri? – I'm not Éri, I say. You are in Paris. This is not Manchester. A mere supposition, nothing I would swear to. Today at noon Manchester may be here for my mother. I was unable to convince her. Éri is in the hospital. *Was soll ich dir sagen?* Éri says nothing. Quick quick my mother spins two threads, two voices, she doubles her money against the Other. Right. I'm not dressed yet says my mother. Props one language against the other. *Ich habe heute Nacht das Buch nicht ausgelesen.* There's a book she didn't finish reading last night, I tell myself. The book that must not end. Éri doesn't answer. *Ich habe heute viel zu tun*, comes the voice of my mother. In the voice I hear the discreet hope of an answer. A conversation might start up again. I hazard a whisper: *Quoi? What?* – I must go and hang out my washing. She says this in French to Éri, therefore to me. Probably I have managed, I don't know how, to be Éri, even if it's in French. So my mother, hastily: *Ich wünsche dir einen guten Tag. Tshüß Éri!* She hangs up fast before the things that Éri doesn't say turn into Éri's Silence. Make a note of this phone call. And the name of the day. The last time on Earth that Ève will have spoken to Éri. I will have forgotten it, I will have thought I was dreaming. The *Ève and Éri* notebook holds a few short questions. This page calls itself "Confusion." But when I find it again, months later, the word Confusion appears to me feeble, hasty, confused. In her Life as an immortal that my mother organizes like a campaign this freezing day will have been the only time my mother will ever have faltered under the scythe. Unless it was she who made the scythe pause. She invented that day. She turned it around, displaced it. Stood in on the spot for the failing actress. Invented the true–false phone call trick. *Keine Wahl.* A hole in the toe of her world through which she risked being whisked to Nothingness, quick she mends it and I am the thread to hand. *Ich wünsche dir einen guten Tag.* I wish you a good day. Never before has anyone played the trick of such a day on me. But what's in a fake? This fake must surely be vital therefore more necessarily true than reality. Am I Éri? Up to a certain question mark. Perhaps. As long as my mother's waking dream lasts. But even in the middle of this grim reaping, she moves on, she clings to her clothesline. There's no witness. I won't tell my mother: you called me Éri. She calls Éri. Éri is in hospital. Never let it be said that my mother didn't succeed in *carrying on* Éri. It was no easy job. I almost tripped her up, in the first instance, I thought I had to defend "reality," I who am on the side of fiction! Luckily I caught myself and for the rest Deafness stepped in. And that's how my two characters invented in a sublime gesture of faithfulness to each other and to themselves, this *Suite.* Later and right up to the day the world has designated as the last and which is the last day of the year, my mother doesn't telephone me any longer to Éri. At least directly. Only a little askew. – Éri, she says to me. – Yes, I say, on December 22. – I think this is the end. One clings to life, providing life is good. She said: I'd rather die. That's her choice. It's not worth it. If there is a price to pay for the life, the life must be worth the price. – Yes, I say. – I made the almond tart and I forgot to put the paper to keep it from sticking. If you make it, don't be careless, put the paper. And saying yes mama, I beg the gods not to leave me in debt. On December 25, she brought in the dry clothes at ten in the morning. Which means she's rising earlier these days. – I'm going to take my shower in a little while. On December 28 she sews the button back on my anorak. There are obstacles. She is having difficulty. – It's not me, it's the old thread. Something about the old thread and the act of sewing comes between her and her will. Her very big hands. Twice as big as mine. Her strength. Ten times mine. Her seriousness. Her thick hair. I am sucking on each second of this holy mass. The sun on the geraniums. She says: Done. A bird chirps. She doesn't hear it. She says: I have an aunt by marriage, Aunt Else, whom nobody likes, not one bit. All the same, it must be said that it was thanks to her that Éri learned to sew. Which always comes in handy. On that day, my mother was being Éri. On December 26, she grows anxious. To think that Éri should be here now. I'd already shopped for her cheeses and her coffee. – Which cheeses? I say. I understand the pain of living. – Boursin and Camembert. We'd better eat them. – I bought a pair of *slippers* – she uses the English word – because I knew hers were worn out. For the slippers, Éri's, what can I say. On the 28th, while we are eating, a half-tear wells on the rim of her left eyelid. This half-tear makes me weep. The whole force of Ève's pain dries during a long silence. We eat. We say nothing. I lose track of my mother behind the curtains of silence. – Ève eats Brussels sprouts and says: Life. It's as long as one has some pleasure. Otherwise it's much too dear. Life. I walk her back home. The walker that serves as her tripod and substitute-automobile is cumbersome. Before we leave the lobby we pause. She puts on her woolen gloves. Struggle of the big hands with the gloves that fight back, escape, stay closed. At last the hands win. Everything is locked up tight. They broke into my neighbor's apartment says my mother, the door. Should I lock the safety lock? If I lock the safety lock no one will be able to get in. I've never locked it. We find ourselves facing a *double bind*. What protects attacks. I say: don't lock it. But my answer doesn't please me. She prepares for bed. Slight limp of the small carcass. The big hands shake. Perhaps it's Éri who doesn't call. Takes a long time turning down the bed. Head in England. Feet on the ground. The big strong hands frail. The television doesn't work. I need to change the batteries in the remote control. She's had the old battery in her purse for ten days. Something keeps her from remembering. Give it to me, I say. This once. To do for her what she can do for herself is an insult. She searches. Doesn't find. It's the day of losing. She dumps out her bag little hankies, papers, keys. Driver's license. Ghost car. The license remains. Not there. It's there. Stashed in a corner. This purse is not practical, I say. – No purse is practical. She throws the purse onto the floor so harshly it skids under the chest of drawers, flat. Éri gave it to me. I kiss her on her left cheek. A scar on her right cheek. Her ears are ringing. Her immense force contained in a tiny patched-up little box. An immense endless fear inhabits me, grins horrors into my ears.

What is Éri in Ève's life? How big a share, how high, how deep, I probe the thin strong nave of the old cathedral, I know nothing of it, is Éri part and parcel of what holds it up? Perhaps she is carved on the outside, statue, figure, metaphor, or could she be inside? On the outside of the inside of every

160

inch of my mother the subtraction spreads its unpredictable toxins. Am I practicing for the next book? Am I aboard the train that my mother loves to take and that I fear? I don't know the final station. End of the year, everyone down.

On December 30, Éri falls asleep. – All right then, good night my daughter my mother says to me. While we are sleeping, Ève and Éri dream the-usual-dumb-dream. They are in the midst of a group of threatening people. Ève says to Éri: all they want *is to disinherit us.* I tried to talk to a policeman says Ève. They wouldn't take me seriously. Éri didn't say anything. I don't know how it ended. I told Éri: the fact that I remember this dream is a sign something is out of joint in my organism. Because I never remember my dreams. But maybe it was Éri's dream. They have invented the Tandem Dream.

On December 31 Ève sorts a year's worth of archives in my drawers. So pretty, busy classifying hundreds of bank statements. Manchester calls. She listens, lost, simple, in the archives. – *I prepared all her cheeses. And then she didn't come.* First in English, then in German. *Ich bin nicht auf der Höhe.* Then in French. *Elle ne voulait pas vivre.* As long as one is alive one doesn't think about not living any longer. What to do? One lights a candle. *As long as one is living one is living.* I make dinner she watches television. Penguins can stay a very long time under water divers breathe with a mask attached to a tube that pipes air to them. Inner Ève can stay for a long time, breathes with a tube, I am the tube but she is the one who gives me air. Suddenly I cry out: mama! I don't see her any more. She's hunched over behind the partition in the little armchair under the window. – I am darning my stockings some holes I made, but I don't have a thimble. Thus my mother brings Éri back. For Éri, ever since 1934, has been everything thread, sewing, hemstitch, cross-stitch, basting, thimble, needles, gathers, darts, mend, overcast. My mother absorbed. She rummages in the sewing box. What's the point of a sewing box without a thimble? At least, I tell myself the without-thimble makes itself strongly felt. One makes do. One still sews. One must overcome the hole. Slowly she puts the needles and the scissors away pondering. *Habe ich jeden Tag telephoniert mit dem Portable. In unserm Alter kann das passieren.* At our age this can happen. I bought a beautiful pair of slippers her chocolates and her cheese. One is all prepared. When that happens however one is not prepared. Socrates leaves us in debt with his cock. My mother owes Éri some cheese and chocolate. What to do? It's like the battery of the trusty old Renault 5 only good to remind me I'm "not in service" only good enough to lend someone younger who's never had an accident, I just had time to unplug it. One is not ready when it happens, still, one is ready.

I scribble these pages while my mother showers. I record the sound of water rippling down my mother for eternity. It is noon. In the coming hour, we sit down to lunch. The thought of Éri too. *Manchester*, says my mother, rhymes with *meine Schwester*, I never thought of that. I never thought she never says "my sister" "*meineSchwester*" I say to myself. Ève says Éri. "My sister" annexes but it separates.

I suggest we drink white wine, I dare, I tremble, Éri likes white wine, I'm afraid of making the wrong choice, should I invite the idea of Éri or avoid it? I feel myself looking for my footing nervously, unsure of the furrow Subtraction has just ploughed through the dining room. One must invent everything. – White wine, not for me, I prefer champagne says my mother you might say Éri is here, for the wine my mother doesn't yield, the Boursin, it's a pity, there isn't any in Manchester, luckily the two sisters agree about the cheese, so Éri will still be here a little, associated with the Parisian cheeses. One eats the cheeses. When we clink glasses it comes to me like a mischievous, soft light that my mother is not about to let herself be *disinherited* either by the cult of memory or by the cult of regret. They have, all the same, slipped through the holes in the net for ninety-six years. Death doesn't interest her, it's like trying to talk to a policeman, life continues to act upon my mother.

At twelve-thirty she steps out of the shower, she beams at me. She lies down on her bed to rest for a moment. This is new. Every day a new battle. After each victory, at once physical and spiritual, she lies down to recoup. The shower too becomes a spiritual enterprise. I can't keep idolatry from nipping at my calves. From her couch mama blares: "I am an old wreck. Still on the road." The sun's path grows shorter and shorter, more and more urgent, we accelerate to keep up, as the hours of wakefulness dwindle things happen one right after the other, I hop aboard, I jump down I race along side by side with mama with life and nothingness at my side. The tone of my tragedy is lightened by peals of laughter. "I'll end up sleeping so long I'll wake up just in time to go to bed, my mother marvels. Sleep *round the clock* you could say: that's untranslatable." She splits her sides chortling around the bed. She makes it with care and curiosity. This bed is full of surprises. Threads of all kinds creep out from under it. She can lose her ears there. No time to be bored *round the clock*. She leads. Blindly I follow. I don't wake her. I wouldn't want to disinherit her of the Sleep world.

"I'm in the avant-garde," says my mother. She thinks me old-fashioned.

She doesn't die. I die me to her, I survive myself to her, I revive myself to her, she dies me, it's my fault, my frailty, my force, the minute she's not in her room, the other is in the stairs, all she has to do is come in, right away my hand comes back to life, I live with a candle. She was the First Backpack, there wasn't even such a thing as a backpack, I was in front, the *Rucksack*, she says in English, later it was all the rage, but before and similarly the concept of Europe already existed in 1920 in Osnabrück, when all the pupils were nationalists, she was the avant-garde of the century with Fraülein von Längeke, I was also in the avant-garde of riding a bicycle without a bar in the middle I got myself insulted in 1950 and now everyone has one, I too thought countries should share sovereignty, I am against delusions of grandeur, Napoleon I detest a really large-scale assassin, hanging Saddam Hussein so out-of-date, everything beautiful has been built with the blood of the wretched, the churches and the castles, we won't mention the present, what a bunch of imbeciles those Americans saddling themselves with a Bush, that lovely city they destroyed everything cultures we're not easy to mix a lot of Israelis are racist too strange when you think of it this mix of easy and difficult, nature needs to be mixed up we don't want to mix or we have to get rid of the collective imagination of cultures, a lead weight on our heads cultures, life that doesn't kill itself so as to live hasn't been invented yet. I am listening to premonitory dreams. I don't have any, do you? What I invented are all those sticks in the windows to keep them from banging. I saw the old broomsticks. I chopped them into pieces fifteen centimeters each. Recycle, before everyone else. I invented avoiding the long way round. I invented making use of the premises rue d'Isly in Algiers after yourfather died. Once you've got the stage, next comes the action. In prison I invented making hair curlers out of carrots. My last time in Oran in 1962 right after the French left there was still *one* shop with sewing things, it came to me, the idea, and I found an extraordinary strawberry-tinted bathrobe, it cost thirty francs what it cost to deliver one baby. As a midwife I took the minimum and for me that was plenty. I didn't want to deal with people with money. All it takes is *one* man to stop a war. In Algeria people had little Moorish babies. This woman said: I don't want her to go to school after she won't want to be a servant, I said: there you have the mindset of stupid people. Yesterday coming out of the super-market a young woman, twenty-four years old, she comes up to me can you spare me some money? I look her: nothing wrong with your health, why don't you get a job? Not one cent. I said. You'll never guess what I found? A ribbon for my typewriter! I fought with my old machine to get the ribbon out. I tried, tried, tried. I plugged away for an hour and I did it. Now I must rest from my labors. I'm going to lie down with the book. That Balzac, I'm amazed what he knew. He knew every kind of human failing. I come to sit beside her bed and I find her amazed: I walked down Rue Sainte-Geneviève, I didn't see the *Pension Vauquer*, have you been there? Now that was a policeman. Who's this Gentleman? That's Vautrin. At the age of forty, he was in that boarding house. Did you know him? Vautrin was a well-known name. He was a great observer obviously better than me. If my mother "sees" this gentleman, the way I "see" him it's that her entire room and us along with it has been transported into realiterature. And to think my mother considers herself, and therefore is, reality personified. All literature inside of her, and her the original whereas in her view literature is the monkey on my back stopping me taking a walk with her. And each time I go for a walk with mama she kindles such a desire in me to take notes, the neighborhood streets race into notebooks unfortunately the more I love her more and more the more I have the urge to leave her, to losefind her through the temptation to get her down in writing, to sketch her, to ask her for paper, to pull words out of her. I invented avoiding the long way round, says my mother. However she is the cause of the detours I can't keep myself from taking because she is herself the Original Detour. When I am about to cut across the Allée Samuel Beckett with my mother as guide and author, the minute we step onto the sidewalk, a book shadows us, we are photographed, the sky through the leaves changes moment by moment, sometimes it is draped in a delicate pink veil, since she's an unconscious author, who never renounces anything, my mother is always in fine fettle, while gazing at the world for the first time at least for that day. I don't tell her that while she's hanging from my left arm, or more precisely sitting like an old hen at the end of the day totting up how much time present or past she has once again earned, economized and saved, my mother plays her part divinely, I see her, I sketch her, I applaud her, occasionally the spectator grows impatient I am bored, I will correct, I won't say act that part again, start that paragraph over, wait a second, say that sentence again, repeat that jab of your cane at the canine dejections, I don't tell her I'm composing the music of her heavy footsteps, a paradoxical version of mama's walking, the slender top, feet in sturdy shoes as ballast for her unstable silhouette. She walks fast and hard like a wiry little statue on a marble base. I record the hushed scuffing of her shuffling slippers and the drumming of the thick shoes.

In the old days I thought I ought to want to fight against the demon my mother sees perched on my shoulder but all that is in the past now, without our being able to want a thing, she poses for me, her life, with advice and recommendations. Thinking about this, I am startled to find myself suspecting that she is jealous of the demon she is for me. Already three in the afternoon. She has just risen. I have been writing since five o'clock this morning. But what is morning, dawn, rise, already, not yet, in realiterature? Here she comes with a glass of orange juice. The terrors hanging in the wardrobe behind me go away. In detail I imagine what strength she must have mustered up in order to fabricate this drink into which she has poured all her hopes of making me forget the world of shadows that the lateness of her appearance has engendered. Trembling she holds out the tall Glass of antidote. – I've lost my scarf she says. – I'm going to find it, I say. –If it is lost, everything is lost she thinks, trembling. I think it's lost she says. – I'll find it, I say. – It's too late says my mother. – But the sun, I say, is still on the mountains and it hasn't finished going down. I stop writing. I'll find the scarf. I am going to get it back.

TRANSLATOR'S NOTES

Remarkable for their experiments with narrative technique, Hélène Cixous's "fictions" (in France it is not thought necessary to affix a genre label) weave narrative, internal monologue, dialogue and discourse, making a fabric whose seams are, deliberately, visible: characters, voices and settings overlap and merge. Sometimes the reader isn't sure who is speaking and where: is it the mother, the daughter, the brother, Balzac, Proust, all or none of the above? Are we in Paris, Algiers, Bordeaux, Athens . . .? Time shifts freely, often abruptly, from past to present, from literary and historical memory to the local market; closure – of chapter, of book – is a momentary stay against confusion.

Naturally, these formal discontinuities are reflected in the language. Critics have commented on Cixous's polysemy, her wit, her plays on and coinages of words, which reveal the "unconscious" of a text; these render her work, at some – indeed, many – levels, untranslatable. (A fertile topic for Cixous research would be the ways language play contributes to the humor that lurks in unexpected places and intensifies, as T.S. Eliot remarked of Andrew Marvell, a text's seriousness.) We can notice how diction abruptly switches register, from the philosophical to the domestic, when, for example, the down-to-earth mother, veering in conversation from mortality to shopping, pulls the figurative carpet out from under the feet of her lyrical-philosophical daughter. One of the challenges, and extraordinary pleasures, of translating Hélène Cixous is encountering and finding linguistic equivalents for the tonal variety in the diction and syntax of the French original.

Another, not unrelated, pleasure is working with the text's poetic elements. Any Cixous text exhibits many of the characteristics of poetry. Sentences pay close attention to rhythm and sound (the translator's word choices will reflect these concerns). Scenes are rich in metaphor – with characteristic comic brio, the first chapter begins: "I threw myself into my study onto my desk, a raft moored to the edge of nothingness in the corner of the door" (p. 1) begins, with characteristic comic brio, *Hemlock*'s first chapter. They expand metonymically, one thing leading to the next via an ever-forking path of associations: in "Henbane," for instance, an allusion to ghosts takes the story down a garden path lushly edged with toxic plants and allusions to *Hamlet*. In a later chapter, "The Vitrine," this associative process is even brought to the surface by the mother when an examination of her cabinet of curiosities leads her to muse:

> [. . .] I really like to think by association, I don't think vertically I think thoughts that touch each other attach spread out join up, it's the best way never to stop, never lose anything find things again, thinks my mother it's very interesting, I begin with one thought and it makes an underground bus I can cross the whole world like this forever

170

getting lost one never knows where one is but one thing leads to another [. . .] . (pp. 52–3)

In this "run-on sentence," which expands to fill most of a page before it stops to catch its breath, the mother, with her characteristic mixture of humility and truculence, is allowed to appropriate a technique that is fundamental to Cixous's narratives, and one whose meanders Cixous, in her Paris Seminars, has tracked in the works of Marcel Proust.

The translator's notes evoke some of the translation's losses and unavoidable detours. Some are difficulties for translations from French into English in general, such as the problem of translating *maman* (see the first note), or translating something as basic as French's "la main" into English's act of possession: "*my* hand"; or the problem of translating out of a language in which nouns are gendered, and verbs and adjectives correspondingly inflected, into English, a difficulty that becomes all the more acute as questions of gender are constantly thematized in Cixous's work, and frequently materialized in wordplays based on the genders of French words. Where the gender of words is important to the context, I have tried to adopt a strategy for translation so as to make this clear. Where strategy has failed I have retreated to an endnote. (Notes are not numbered in the text. They will be found, collected chapter by chapter, below.)

Another difficulty for translators working from contemporary French works whose tone is conversational is the French third-person impersonal pronoun *on*, or "one," which, to English ears, especially American English ears, may sound stilted. The French "one" may be translated into English using, as appropriate, all the other pronouns and, of course, "one." I have translated it variously, according to context and function. But I have preferred, as is mentioned in a note to the last chapter, "Éri Goes On Ahead," to keep "one" when

171

its use signals, often humorously, the author's questioning of the very idea of a coherent speaking voice, or a character's attempt to distance or displace herself from a fraught situation. A telling instance of this emerges from the level of the implicit to the explicit in Cixous's *The Day I Wasn't There* (tr. Beverley Bie Brahic, Evanston, IL: Northwestern University Press, 2006, p. 83), when the narrator, absent at the time of her son's death, questions her mother about the burial:

> It wasn't a burial, says my mother. [. . .] There was a wall filled with pigeonholes for all the little children. One puts them in *a box*. [. . .] One took him to the Jewish cemetery,
> "Who was *One*? I wondered. Was it my mother?

No change in syntax is without its effect: I confess to feeling a nagging unease whenever I translate a "passive" sentence into English's preferred active voice because I know how this changes the emphasis. Similarly in the case of reflexive pronouns ("*Je m'endors* . . . I put myself to sleep . . . I fall asleep"), more common in French and sometimes employed by Cixous (see the note to "Éri Goes On Ahead") in her own manner, often in order to draw attention to the reflexivity of an action, thus rendering action, thought and language doubly "foreign." Translation is a matter of trial and error, of totting up gains on one side and losses on the other. One word may be preferred to another seemingly equally good one, in the original as in the translation, as a result of a (somewhat intuitive) weighing of alternatives; perhaps a three-syllable word beginning with "b" sounded better in that slot . . . .

Of course, the question of whether a translator should endeavor to keep an "accent" of the source language (French, here) and culture in the target language (English, here) has been debated from Dryden to Nabokov, Hölderlin to Benjamin; translation, the argument in favor of respecting foreignness goes, contributes to the evolution of languages and cultures, and a too "transparent" translation may, by smoothing out the original so as to adapt it to the cultural norms of target-language readers, constitute an act of appropriation by a dominant culture, and at the same time deprive that culture of a productive encounter with "otherness." One way of enabling such evolution is to import some of the syntax or idioms of the source language – which, after all, reflect the way a language thinks, and which, translators and theorists claim, may be betrayed by being invisibly stitched into a "fluent" translation. French deploys verb tenses differently, its sentences (positioning of phrases, clauses, adverbs, adjectives, etc.) are constructed differently, its punctuation is different (punctuating French dialogue in the English manner would considerably change the feel of a translation; punctuating it in the French manner has enlarged the field of dialogue in contemporary English fiction; what English considers a "run-on sentence" in search of a semi-colon may be tolerated, or more lightly punctuated, in French, and so forth). About Cixous's idiosyncratic punctuation, more below. Her syntax too is often experimental as she attempts to capture thoughts and feelings in the process of being thought and felt; her sentences with their rapid, sometimes seemingly inexplicable tense shifts, their ellipses and fragmentation, their shifting pronouns contribute to the astounding immediacy of her books. The truth is that Cixous's writing can sound foreign, even in French. This translation aspires to have the same lively strangeness as the original.

A word about punctuation. I have respected the punctuation or its lack in the French text, except where this made the English text ambiguous – in a bad way (there's lots of deliberate ambiguity here). Hélène Cixous herself says that with regard to speech tags, the more "correctly" they are punctuated the more conscious the speaker: that is, the closer she is to the surface, and the more lightly punctuated these tags are, the more the speaker is inside herself, in a dream-like state. The punctuation of her texts, she says, reflects the many layers of the character's consciousness (the character being multiple people at once, thinking on multiple levels): "'Hélène Cixous' is a character who is a writer and who is always thinking about writing, writing about writing, writing in her thoughts, even while she does other things, she is very self-reflexive about the process of writing. Sometimes she thinks thoughts and other times she thinks 'sentences'" (HC, personal communication, November 2008).

Readers interested in pursuing this matter may wish to consult Jacques Derrida's book *H.C. for Life, That Is to Say* (tr. Laurent Milesi and Stefan Herbrechter, Stanford, CA: Stanford University Press, 2006), a tribute to Cixous's writing which, among other things, explores the intricacies of her punctuation.

One last comment: on Cixous's creative method. I alluded above to her use of associative slides between contiguous elements, a technique made explicit by one of the mother's musings. In *Hemlock* ("To Have to Lose"), the daughter-writer also comments on her habit of jotting down everything *immediately* in her notebooks – the notebooks (no French pupil escapes a *cahier* fetish), purchased half-price at the supermarket by the thrifty mother or offered her by friends coming back from their travels, that are made so tangible in book after Cixous book. In "To Have to Lose," the daughter, in despair over her hard-of-hearing mother's failure to catch a word, resorts to writing it on a scrap of paper:

> And when my mother stares at the Paper, there is a blank
> [. . .] of which I immediately take note. [. . .] for if one lets
> the wave pass, if one doesn't right away yoke oneself to the
> trace, if one doesn't throw oneself heart and soul after the

invisible animal, abandoning all other business, if one lets oneself be turned from the essential by society, despite all the recommendations, forever vain, of the prophet within me who foretells the whale within me, the event without a name vanishes, slipping away as powerfully as a dream and all the more imperceptibly as it seems insignificant. (p. 135)

A comment I wish to link here to a Lacanian observation (in the preface to "The Function and Field of Speech and Language in Psychoanalysis"): "Nothing created appears without urgency; nothing in urgency fails to surpass itself in speech" (*Écrits: The First Complete Edition in English*, tr. Bruce Fink, New York: W.W. Norton, 2006, p. 127).

I am grateful to Peggy Kamuf for her reading of these Translator's Notes and for her own inspiring translations, and to Hélène Cixous for her reading of the translation-in-progress and her elucidations of words, sentences, sections over which I dithered, and also for her tolerance of questions such as "Does your mother sleep on the ground floor?" and "Is the bathroom upstairs?" – questions not strictly speaking necessary for the translating of a passage, but essential to my mental vision of a setting-in-translation. I am solely responsible for all errors – there are bound to be some – of omission and commission.

MAMA'S NOT IN MAMA – THERE'S SOMEONE ELSE

Mama (p. 1): it is hard to settle on a translation for the French *maman*: mama, mum, mom, momma, mama . . . ? All these have sociocultural, age and/or geographic overtones, where the French *maman* is more universal, used from (the speaker's) childhood to maturity, across social classes. I have chosen "mama," in part because I liked it in the work of another translator (Peggy Kamuf), in part because it has (for me) some of the tenderness and sounds of *maman*.

"Disappearance" [. . .] I've seen her – I saw it" (p. 1): in French *disparition* is feminine, leading to ambiguity about the gender of "disappearance," here personified, when the narrator says *"je l'ai vue."*

bibliomortgaged (p. 2): *bibliohypothéqué*, an invented word.

her music (p. 8): in the sense of her "song and dance," her "routine" (HC)

neither two nor one (p. 10): among other sources, see Shakespeare's "The Phoenix and the Turtle": "So they lov'd as love in twain / [...] Single nature's double name / Neither two nor one was call'd."

IN WHICH COUNTRY

still [. . .] left behind (p. 12): *reste* in French, what remains. It recurs – like a lament – in this passage, but unfortunately no single English word fits both contexts, and *reste que* has been translated as "still."

four dream colors red white black and rome (p. 12): in addition to being the name of the city, "rome" (the same word is used in French) as an anagram is a homophone for *more* (death).

between the end and the last time (p. 19): between the time Socrates was put in prison and his death (HC).

Vautrin (p. 25): Vautrin is the name of a convict-police chief character in Balzac's novels, including in *Le Père Goriot*. Note also the recurrence of the letters or sound "vau" in this passage, in the names as well as in French expressions such as *il vaut mieux* ("I'd better"), from French *valoir* ("value, to be worth"); *veau* (veal); *vautour* (vulture). See also Jacques Lacan, *Écrits* [tr. Bruce Fink, New York: Norton, 2002], "The Instance of the Letter in the Unconscious": "Freud shows us in every possible way that the image's value as a signifier has nothing to do with its signification, giving as an example Egyptian hieroglyphics in which it would be ridiculous to deduce from the frequency in a text of a vulture (which is an aleph) or a chick (which is a vau) indicating a form of the verb 'to be' and plurals, that the text has anything whatsoever to do with these ornithological specimens [. . .]" (p. 151).

HENBANE

the damned juice of jusquiame, *henbane* (p. 35): jusquiame is another name for henbane, or "hebenon," in *Hamlet*, Act I, scene v: "Upon my secure hour thy uncle stole, / With juice of cursed hebenon in a vial, / And in the porches of my ears did pour / The leperous distilment;"

See also Yves Bonnefoy's essay on Mallarmé, "La hantise du ptyx," in *L'Imaginaire métaphysique* (Paris: Seuil, 2006), pp. 108-9: "'Hebenon'! Translating the tragedy, encountering this word, searching among the editors of *Hamlet* and other commentators of Shakespeare for a plausible explanation for this vocable of no known language, forced to conclude there isn't one, I confess that I, for my part, heard there once again the old tempter, the badly-buried demon, murmur that 'hebenon' [. . .] is the resurgence of the inaccessible second degree of language, which lets itself be approached perhaps,

in some decisive moments of the anxious human search"
(pp. 108–9).

PUT ME A GHOST AT THE EMBARCADERO

The French chapter title is *M'être un fantôme à L'Embarcadère*.
M'être is a coined reflexive verb, suggesting "to be to oneself,"
but one may also hear *mettre* ("to put").

Leytter (p. 38): *Leytre* in French, a combination of the name
of a river, the Leyre, near Arcachon, and the word "letter"
(HC).

fiery porch (p. 41): *porche ardent* in French. A *chapelle ardente*
is a mortuary chapel, because of the candles.

the Allée Samuel Beckett (p. 43): This is the name of the
median strip, or promenade, with benches and trees, that runs
down the Avenue René Coty between Denfert-Rochereau
and the Parc Montsouris in Paris's 14th Arrondissement.
Samuel Beckett lived in the 14th Arrondissement at the end
of his life. Several times in the course of the story the narrator crosses this median strip, going or returning to her own
apartment from her mother's apartment.

the narrator of the useless automobile (p. 43): the narrator
of Proust's *Albertine disparue* (*Albertine Gone*).

THE VITRINE

The French title is *La Vie Trine*, in which the reader hears the
name of the piece of furniture that features in this chapter, a
vitrine (glass cabinet for bric-à-brac), but also *Vie* ("life") and
Trine, a coinage suggesting "three . . . triple . . . trinity" (HC).

my mother trusts, trusts her daughter (p. 51): *ma mère se fie, fiée absolument à sa fille*, plays on the similar sounds of *fier* and *fille*.

the swerves of the conversation (p. 61): the original text adapts the expression *coq-à-l'âne*, or "cock-to-ass," used as an image for a conversation in which there are abrupt changes of subject.

***Oh horrible! Oh horrible! Most horrible!* (p. 61):** in English in the original.

Champs-Élysées (p. 62): the avenue, but also the Elysium Fields.

TWO SLICES OF LIFE

between the slices of pine (p. 70): *entre les tranches de pin*, which in French sounds like *entre les tranches de pain* (bread).

I read around these edges (p. 76): *Je lis autour de ces bordages*, in French. *Le bord* is the edge, the brink. *Bordage* can be a sewing term for "edging," a nautical term for "planking," or a metallurgical term for "plating." One might also hear *abordage*, a nautical term for "boarding" in the sense of climb aboard; or the verb *border (un lit)*, meaning "to tuck in."

HEMLOCK

nightfall (p. 80): *la tombée (du jour)* in French. Although Hélène Cixous said she intended *la tombée du jour*, the word also, of course, evokes *tombe* (tomb).

179

whether I side with him [. . .] or whether I go along with my mother (p. 81): in French *si je le suis [. . .] où si je suis ma mere*. *Suis* from the verb *suivre*, "to follow, to go along with," but also perhaps from the verb *être*, "to be": *je suis*, "I am".

the setting of the Sun (p. 83): *le couchement du soleil*. *Couchement* is a coinage formed from the radical of the verb *coucher* (to lie or lay down) and the suffix *-ment*; *couchement* emphasizes the ongoingness of the action; it also calls to mind Ève's work as a midwife, for *accouchement* is the French word for the process of giving birth: labor and delivery.

luxuries [. . .] oblivious of time's claws (p. 88): *luxe [. . .] les griffes du temps*. *Griffes* means "claws," but it also means a (designer) label.

COUSIN DEAFNESS

Catching the sea in a net (p. 91): *Retenir la mer dans un filet*. *La mer* means "the sea"; *la mère*, its homophone, means "mother." This is a play on words which, not surprisingly, recurs often in this and other Cixous books.

Meanwhile she who delivered me reads on (p. 93): the French text, *Et pendant ce temps celle qui m'a livrée, lit*, contains a play on *livre* ("book"), *lit* ("reads," but also "bed") and *livrer* ("to deliver").

THE JERK

Denfert (p. 98): Denfert-Rochereau is the name of a metro stop in the 14th Arrondissement of Paris. Hidden inside it is *enfer*, which means "hell" in French.

rhapsody (p. 98): from Greek *rhapsōidia*, from *rhaptein* "to stitch" + *ōidē* "song, ode."

Me and my life. My life and my death. (p. 100): the French says *Ma vie et moi. Ma vie et ma mort. Et* means "and" but it also sounds like "is."

Can dreams, then, predict the future? (p. 105): see Freud's *The Interpretation of Dreams*, Appendix A, "A Premonitory Dream Fulfilled" (tr. James Strachey (New York: Avon, 1965), pp. 661–4.

there – have – yet to be seen – (p. 106): there is a wordplay in French here on the homophones *avoir* ("to have") and *à voir* ("to be seen").

Who-is-death, my friend J.D. says (p. 106): *A Qui-est-la mort*, see Jacques Derrida, *Demeure, Athènes* (Paris: Galilée, 2009), p. 157.

the logbook (p. 106): *la lèvre du bord*, in French, a play on the similarity between the words *lèvre* ("lip") and *livre* ("book").

You know when the theory starts, says mybrother, there's no end in sight (p. 107): The same words are used by Jacques Derrida in his text *Demeure, Athènes*, pp. 34–5.

ave (p. 107): in French "ave" stands on its own, but is also joined to *nir* in the next line. *Ave + nir = avenir*, or "future."

"We are owed to death" (p. 114): Jacques Derrida, in *Demeure, Athènes*, pp. 52ff., talks about the difficulty of understanding, and of translating, the phrase "Nous nous devons à la mort." See also Catherine Malabou, Jacques Derrida and David Wills, *Counterpath* [Stanford: Stanford University Press, 2004], chapter 7, "The Greek Delay": "The text *Demeure, Athènes* ('Nous nous devons à la mort') was written to accompany a series of photographs and is entirely devoted to an analysis of the delay effect, to a type of inopportunity or contretemps, the non-coincidence of self with self, or of self with other" (p. 103).

***Once again the ungraspable* (p. 115):** from Proust's note-books (HC).

"[like those images called up by a music that seems unable to contain them]" (p. 115): from Proust's notebooks (HC).

according to Derrida "Manche sait se taire" (p. 116): from Jacques Derrida, "Telepathy" and *The Post Card* (HC). Note also *manche* ("handle"), *La Manche* (the English Channel) . . . Manchester, the home of the narrator's Aunt Éri. Cixous also refers to Derrida's pun in *Philippines* (tr. Laurent Milesi, Cambridge: Polity, 2010).

my tongue (p. 116): in French *la langue* is both the "tongue" (in the mouth) and the "language," even the "mother-tongue."

Françoise (p. 116): *Françoise* is the name of the housekeeper-cook in Proust's *In Search of Lost Time*.

GET, GOTCHA

A faith, once God disappeared (p. 120): *une foi, une fois Dieu disparu.* The French plays on the homophony of *une foi* ("a faith") and *une fois* ("once").

For all the good it did him (p. 121): *Ça lui a fait une belle jambe* is a French expression. Here it allows Cixous, in French, to play on *jambe* (leg) and *jambon* ("ham").

TO HAVE TO LOSE

the abyss brought about by the unlikely but stormy grandeur of the disaster (p. 130): the following paragraphs contain a great deal of sea (*mer/mère*) imagery, evoking storms, whales and difficult crossings.

I say: Jonas (p. 137): Jonas is the French spelling of the biblical Jonah.

surreptitiously disobedient (p. 139): Cixous's linguistic compression is lost in translation here, for the word she uses in French is *dérobéissante*, which compacts several words into a single, made-up word. In *dérobéissante* one hears *désobéissante* ("disobedient"), *dérober* ("to steal, rob"), *dérobé* ("hidden, concealed, secret") and *robe* ("robe, dress").

But sitting on the shores of my mother, my body of water (p. 141): the *mère/mer* imagery returns here in Cixous's phrase, *Mais assise au bord de ma mère*, expanded to make the imagery more explicit in English. Note also "the depths," "without a compass," "a black oilcloth sea" (*la toile d'une mer noire cirée*), "sheets of water" and the Jonas family epic.

THE BLUE NOTEBOOK

Hélène put her foot down. Or put it off until tomorrow (p. 148): the French text, *Hélène a refusé de main de maître. Ou demain de mettre, ou de naître*, plays with the sounds of *de main*, *demain*, *maître*, *mettre* and *naître*, none of which the English text has captured.

Then, quick, death does its work (p. 154): from Wilhelm Busch's *Max and Moritz*: "First Trick."

Ève is able to do the little geraniums, without reading without lyre (p. 155): *Ève peut les petits geraniums, sans lire, sans lyre*, with a play on the homophony of *lire* and *lyre*.

Venice . . . Life . . . Ève (p. 155): in French these sounds echo – *Venise . . . Vie . . . Ève*.

ÉRI GOES ON AHEAD

But what's in a fake? (p. 158): this passage plays on the similar sounds and dissimilar meanings of two French words, (*le*) *faux* ("fake, the fake") and *la faux* ("scythe").

As long as one is alive one doesn't think about not living any longer. What to do? One lights a candle (p. 161): a difficulty of translating from French to English is knowing when the impersonal third-person pronoun *on* ("one") should be translated by "one" (which can sound overly formal in conversational English) and when it is more appropriate to use "they," "we" or even "I." Here, as at times elsewhere, the distancing or displacement effect of the mother speaking of her own thoughts and actions in the third person is very important to the tone of the passage, as to the psychology of the mother and the daughter's perception and portrayal of the mother.

She's hunched over behind the partition in the little armchair under the window (p. 161): there are, in fact, three principal settings in the story, the mother's apartment on one side of the Allée Samuel Beckett, the daughter's apartment on the other side and a house in the country where they cohabit, mainly during vacation time.

She doesn't die. I die me to her, I survive myself to her, I revive myself to her, she dies me (p. 163): *Elle ne meurt pas. Je me meurs à elle, je me survis à elle, je me revis d'elle, elle me meurt.* This may be an appropriate place to mention the difficulty of translating French reflexive verbs and their pronouns into English, even if *se mourir* is not, of course, a common reflexive, but one which is strange, even in French, whence its power.

As a learner of French, a schoolchild quickly learns to translate a locution like *je me lave les mains* into "I wash my hands," taking for granted the strange *me*: "I [me/myself] wash [the/my] hands. But these "strangenesses" of the foreign language, if they are highlighted by a writer such as Cixous, acquire a weight that is hard to ignore. And even the ordinary usage suggests something untranslatable about the way the French language "thinks."

I didn't see the *Pension Vauquer* (p. 165): the *Pension Vauquer* is in Balzac's novel *Le Père Goriot*. See also "Vautrin" note above, *In Which Country*.

185